Jamie Buckir

The Journey to...
SPIRITUAL MATURITY

Following the Footsteps of Moses in the Sinai Peninsula

A WORKBOOK to be used with the 13-Lesson Video Tape Series

The Journey to Spiritual Maturity Workbook
By Jamie Buckingham

Copyright © 2014, 2017 by Risky Living Ministries, Inc.
Original publication: 1988

Scripture references, unless otherwise noted, are taken from the *New International Version*. Used by permission. All rights reserved worldwide.

Published by Risky Living Ministries, Inc.
3901 Hield Road NW
Palm Bay, Florida, 32907
www.rlmin.com

Risky Living Ministries is dedicated to preserving the life works of Jamie Buckingham.

ISBN: 978-1494965525

The Journey to Spiritual Maturity Workbook

Following the Footsteps of Moses

By

Jamie Buckingham

THE JOURNEY TO SPIRITUAL MATURITY
FOLLOWING THE FOOTSTEPS OF MOSES
WITH
JAMIE BUCKINGHAM

CONTENTS

GETTING THE MOST OUT OF THIS STUDY
- Lesson 1. INTRODUCTION TO THE SINAI
- Lesson 2. PURGING: THE WATERS OF MARAH
- Lesson 3. PROVISION: FILLED WITH THE SPIRIT
- Lesson 4. OBEDIENCE: WATER FROM THE ROCK
- Lesson 5. AUTHORITY: COMING INTO SUBMISSION
- Lesson 6. CHANGED APPETITES: MANNA FROM HEAVEN
- Lesson 7. RESTORATION: SPIRITUAL DOMINION
- Lesson 8. THE CALL OF GOD: THE BURNING BUSH
- Lesson 9. HOSPITALITY: LEARNING TO GIVE
- Lesson 10. THE LAW: LESSONS FROM MT. SINAI
- Lesson 11. PILGRIMS: STAYING UNDER THE CLOUD
- Lesson 12. FAITH: LESSONS FROM KADESH BARNEA
- Lesson 13. RELATIONSHIPS: THE FAMILY OF GOD

NOTES

The Journey to Spiritual Maturity
PREFACE

We live in a hurry-up world, a world of electronics, computers, and videos. Reading, especially reading to study and learn, is rapidly becoming a thing of the past. It's not that we don't want to read. It's just hard to find the time to do it any more.

At the same time, there is a resurgence of desire on the part of a number of serious Christians to learn more about the ways of God. Christians want to know more about the God they love, more about His plan for their lives, more of His program designed to move them into spiritual maturity. In short, we want to be "conformed to the image of Christ."

This video series on "The Journey to Spiritual Maturity" has been designed to meet that need — using video and the written word — i.e, this workbook. The workbook has been prepared for classroom use. Ideal usage calls for a group of people who want to move on to spiritual maturity to commit themselves to meet for 13 sessions — probably once a week — with a teacher. Each session should last an hour — although it could be stretched out for a longer period of time if the group agrees. The group should view the video at the beginning of the class. (Each video section runs for about 12 minutes — a few shorter, some a bit longer.) Then the teacher will take over and, using this workbook as a guide, lead the class in a study of the material at hand.

The material is ideally suited for use by a Sunday school class, for home group study, or even by a family who wants to spend regular time in Bible study. Although it has been prepared primarily for class use, the material can be used just as easily by an individual or a couple without a teacher — however the ideal method is to study the material in a group else you lose the benefit of interaction by being in the presence of others who are learning by asking questions.

The video material was taped "on location" in the Sinai peninsula. It is the climax of seven, two-week research trips I have made into the Sinai over a period of years. On this particular trip I took a group of ten men with me — as well as a camera crew. Each man in the group was on his own journey to spiritual maturity as we traced the footsteps of Moses and the Children of Israel as they made their way from Egypt to Canaan — 3,200 years ago. At various points along the way we paused in our journey and I taught the group on some phase of spiritual maturity. Later I edited the material into the video teaching sessions you will be using in this class.

I am indebted to Michael Little of the Christian Broadcasting Network who originally commissioned this series, and to Peter Darg, Middle East correspondent for CBN,

NOTES

NOTES

who accompanied me on my last trip, as head cameraman, producer, and editor. I am also indebted to Bruce Braun who helped with additional taping and editing here in the States and to John French of Scottsdale, Arizona — one of the pilgrims who accompanied me on that trip — who had the vision to put this package together.

Unlike some of the current "teaching videos" — which are little more than talking heads on a TV screen — this one is designed to be used with a live teacher. The video segments do not give answers. Their purpose is to interest the student in the subject to be studied, to give him some insight into Biblical geography with a "you are there" feel, and to stimulate questions and a desire for further study.

I hope you learn as much as I did when I retraced the footsteps of Moses — and I hope you have as much fun learning from video and the Bible as I did trudging through the sand and climbing those mountains you'll see on the TV screen during these 13 sessions we spend together.

Jamie Buckingham
Melbourne, Florida

GETTING THE MOST OUT OF THIS STUDY

Using the accompanying video tapes this workbook is designed to lead you, step by step, deeper into spiritual maturity. The Introduction and each of the other 12 lessons begins with a brief video presentation from the Sinai, giving you an opportunity to "follow the footsteps of Moses," walking where he walked and learning the lessons he learned. By video you will become part of a small group of men who stopped at various places along the path of Moses and listened as I taught. You will meet some of the people who currently live in the Sinai — Bedouins, whose ancestors lived in this very place 3,200 years ago where Moses and the Children of Israel crossed this same wilderness on their way to the Promised Land. The lessons learned by those early pilgrims are still valid today. Those lessons will become our guideposts, helping us as we make our way through our own wildernesses on our way to that place called spiritual maturity.

The material on the video tape and in the workbook can be used in a number of different ways. It can be the basis of an individual study or be used in a Sunday school class or a house group setting over a number of weeks. Experience has shown the greatest benefit will come when a group of people study the material together under a leader who is well-prepared on the subject.

Helps for the Leader

If you are a leader preparing to take a group of people on their journey to spiritual maturity, you should consider the following:

1. Necessary Materials

A good color television set large enough to be seen by all present.

A video tape player.

A power source within reach of the plugs for the TV and VCR.

Comfortable seating so each person may see the TV screen and teacher.

A Bible for each student.

A workbook for each student.

Pen or pencil for each student.

2. Preparation

Before teaching others you should not only view the entire video series — all 13 segments — but you should work your way through this workbook. You will find a number of scripture references. Study them in depth before attempting to lead the class in discussion. You are not expected to have all the answers. Your job will be to help the students ask the right questions and stimulate them to explore the Bible for themselves.

3. Be Aware

As you lead the class be aware that each person present is going through some kind of personal wilderness. This could be a financial crisis, a grief experience, a problem with personal identification, a battle with temptation, a crisis in the home, spiritual confusion, or a number of different mountains which seem too high to climb and too thick to tunnel through. Your awareness of their pilgrimage will help when it comes to answering their questions and leading them in discussion.

4. Stick to the Subject

As on all journeys there will be a temptation to chase rabbits which will lead you off the main trail and into a maze of irrelevant material. It is important you stick, as nearly as possible, to the outline of the subject at hand. The material has been carefully designed to build principle on principle with the eventual aim of the student becoming "thoroughly equipped for every good work" (II Timothy 3:17). Do not preach. Do not monopolize the conversation. Do not allow the class to drift away from the subject matter.

5. Stimulate Discussion

Remember, your job as teacher is not to give answers, but to stimulate discussion and encourage each student to find God's direction for his own life as he makes his personal pilgrimage from the bondage of Egypt to the Promised Land of spiritual maturity. Do not limit yourself to the material covered in the workbook. It is merely a guide, a primer for discussion. Allow the Holy Spirit to direct your class sessions.

6. Be Sensitive to Time

If your class has more than an hour for each study, arrange for a break of a few minutes for refreshments or a stretch. If the group discussion is vital, or if someone in the class indicates a need for personal ministry, you may want to keep the session going. Or, if the particular subject is stimulating extra discussion, you may want to put off the next segment in order to continue this one for an additional week. If that is the case, you may want to show the video for that particular segment a second time when you meet again.

Helps for Students

Before you start this course ask yourself these questions: Am I really committed to moving on to spiritual maturity? Am I willing to commit myself to attending all 13 sessions of this course unless unavoidably detained? Am I willing to prepare ahead of time through prayer and by reading my Bible and doing my workbook? Am I willing to enter into the group discussion — asking questions and expressing my personal opinions?

If you answered "no" to any of these questions you should reconsider whether you should take this course. If you answered "yes" to all questions you are ready to proceed. Here are some immediate steps you can take to insure maximum benefit from the course.

1. Set Goals

This course is designed to help you move on into spiritual maturity. It does not matter whether you are young or old, a seasoned Christian or a new convert. Each of us needs to go beyond where we are, and the principles learned over these next 13 sessions will help you move from where you are spiritually into a deeper walk with God. Look ahead to where you want to be. What kind of Christian do you desire to be? What kind of Christian do you believe God wants you to be? Set a goal and let this study help you get there.

2. Honestly Evaluate Your Present Condition

Where are you as a Christian? Are you still in the bondage of Egypt, enslaved by the habits of this world? Have you made a commitment to follow Jesus regardless of the cost? Do you fear the journey? Perhaps you've started but have gotten bogged down and confused by seeming complexities of the Christian life. Or maybe your desire remains strong but circumstances keep sucking at you like desert quicksand, so for every step you take forward it seems you take two back. Honestly evaluate your present condition as you begin this next step on your journey toward spiritual maturity, for without a willingness to face yourself it will be impossible to understand what God is saying for your life.

Your faith commitment to follow this course and become the person God intends you to be must not only be pursued but it should stand the bright light of constant measurement and self-inventory. You know the kind of person you already are. You know the level of commitment you already display. The question you must now face is not "Can I do it?", but, "Am I willing to commit to place myself in a position where God can do it in me?"

At the end of each chapter there is a place where you — in the privacy of your own study — can evaluate your personal progress. The answers you give to the questions will give you some kind of spiritual indicator as to your progress week by week. The questions will also help fix the Word of God more firmly in your heart, and thus provide a reservoir of truth that the Holy Spirit can draw upon in the training and shaping of your life.

3. You'll Not Pass This Way Again

Although God gives us infinite chances to improve and move into spiritual maturity, if you do not take advantage of each opportunity you will find it increasingly difficult to respond the next time around the mountain. Thus when discussion in the class opens the door for you to express yourself and ask for personal ministry, do not hesitate to respond. Remember, the Children of Israel all left Egypt with the expectation of entering the Promised Land. However, all but two of them died in the wilderness because they failed to respond when they had a chance to obey. Don't let pride or fear of criticism keep you from moving on. Only those who ask questions receive answers. Only those who seek help find it. Only those who request the filling of the Holy Spirit are filled.

4. Study Each Chapter Before Class

Ideally, you should study each chapter in this workbook *before* coming to class. Look up each Scripture reference, answer all the questions by filling in the blanks and circling the true/false answers. For instance, after viewing the opening session on video — the Introduction to the Sinai — you should take this workbook home and study Lesson 2: PURGING. This way, when it is time for the next class session, you will be prepared to view the video and take part in the discussion. Of course, if it is impossible to study ahead of time, you should still take part in the class activities.

NOTES

5. Set Your Own Pace

One of the lessons the pilgrim learns as he makes his way through the wilderness is this: God's patience is infinite as long as you are moving with Him. The only time you get left behind is when you determine you want to go no farther on your spiritual quest. Do not be afraid to move slowly. To rush through this study may mean you learn all the right religious answers but miss the real lessons God wants to teach you. The course is designed to provoke you to your own searching and thinking, and to a demonstration of faith in God.

6. Check Your Progress

Once you have completed the course, ask your pastor or group leader to sit down with you and review your answers — and your spiritual progress. Remember: "testing," in the Biblical sense, is not an examination of how much you have learned. Rather it is God's opportunity to teach you through experience. Thus when God "tested" the Children of Israel at Marah (you'll study this in Lesson Two) He was actually teaching them through the circumstances. A final individual "test" at the hands of your pastor or group leader will help you assimilate what you have learned and give you some indication of the next steps needed in your journey to spiritual maturity.

NOTE: Unless otherwise stated Scripture quotations are taken from the New International Version, copyright 1978 by New York International Bible Society and published by the Zondervan Corporation, Grand Rapids, Michigan. Used by permission. Each chapter has a number of questions with accompanying Scripture references. By looking up the references you should be able to answer all the questions. Do not be ashamed to fill in the blanks — even if you give the wrong answer. No one is going to grade you. The questions are given to emphasize important principles and facts. By looking up the answers you will learn. Go ahead, try it. It's fun to learn — especially when you are learning about God.

Lesson 1
Introduction to the Sinai

VIDEO REFERENCE: Lesson 1

Although very few of us will ever spend time in a desert, and almost none of us will ever wander in one as Moses and the Children of Israel did, wilderness experiences are common to all of us. The conflicts faced by those early Israelites — 3,200 years ago, as they left Egypt on their trek through the Sinai toward a Promised Land — still beset us all. Fear. Uncertainty. Grief. Anger. Doubt. Discouragement. Temptation. These are the constant companions of all of us on our pilgrim journey from the bondage of sin (or the bondage of dead religion) to the freedom of spiritual maturity.

There is a tendency, when we come to the end of ourselves, to accuse others — and sometimes accuse God — for our problems. Yet, if we remain in the wilderness long enough, we eventually realize God allowed us to wander in order to purge us of all our yesterdays and prepare us for the wonderful things in store for us tomorrow. That is the purpose of the wilderness: to purge and to prepare. And to allow us to get quiet enough to meet and have fellowship with God.

In our grief, confusion, faltering faith, sin or adversity, we may wander as the lost Children of Israel. Or we may discover that the wilderness is the point of our true beginning with God.

Even as with the Children of Israel, the choice is ours — to wander, or to faithfully follow God's leading into the promised new life of spiritual maturity.

The Sinai is such a wilderness. It remains today as it was 3,200 years ago when the Children of Israel entered — following more than 400 years of slavery in Egypt on their way to the Promised Land of Canaan. In my own treks through this barren wilderness, I have found, as they did, a rough land of beauty — a crucible that fashions saints or madmen from those who dare to venture out. I have returned again and again, drawn by the wisdom and restorative powers I've found there.

Traveling through the land of the Exodus — at fireside with the desert people who still live there, the Bedouin, climbing the tortuous paths up Mt. Sinai, beside the

NOTES

bitter waters of Marah and in the cosmic silence and solitude of a wilderness night — I've learned ancient Bible truths that have forever altered my life. I discovered, as you will, that it is God Himself who welcomes and guides the lost, weary, foot-sore and soul-hungry wanderers.

In this video introduction to the Sinai, I want you to begin to get the feel of the desert. Only as we go "on location" will we fully understand the impact the wilderness made on those early Israelite pilgrims. Then, as we study each chapter together, the lessons God taught them will become our lessons also. Hopefully we will emerge from this study much closer to our goal of spiritual maturity than we were when we entered.

If not, well, we can always circle the mountain again.

CONCLUSIONS

1. God wants to set us free from the bondage of sin and legalism (Egypt) and move us into spiritual maturity (Canaan).

2. The only way to get to our desired goal is through the wilderness.

3. No situation can ever come into the life of a believer which has not first passed through the hands of God — and thus has redeeming quality.

4. The purpose of the wilderness is to purge us of the past and prepare us for the future.

BIBLE STUDY

1. The book of Genesis closes with the story of Joseph and his brothers, all children of old Jacob whose name had been changed to Israel. These "Children of Israel" had made their home in Eygpt due to a famine in their original homeland of Canaan (now modern-day Israel). In Egypt due primarily to Joseph's influence with the Pharaoh, the Israelites were honored guests. But things changed across the years following the death of Joseph.

   Why did the Egyptian Pharaoh put the Israelites in slavery?
   (Exodus 1:8-10)

   _____

   _____

   _____

2. After more than 400 years of slavery, a baby was born to a Hebrew couple and raised in the house of Pharaoh. This baby, Moses, grew to be a man of great power and influence in Egypt. Then at the age of 40 he discovered his Hebrew ancestry.

   Why was Moses driven into the wilderness? (Exodus 2:11-15)

   _____

   _____

   _____

3. At the end of a 40 year period in the wilderness, Moses heard a voice from God speaking from a burning bush near Mt. Sinai. As far as we know, it was the first time in 400 years that the Lord had confronted one of His chosen people.

   What did God tell Moses from the burning bush? (Exodus 3:10)

   _____

   _____

   _____

4. When Moses returned to Israel, at the age of 80, he confronted the Eygptian Pharaoh. Following a series of plagues, the Children of Israel were released and allowed to enter the wilderness on their way to Canaan. However, even before they were able to get out of Egypt, they came face to face with a seemingly impossible barrier — the northern waters of the Gulf of Suez, which is an extension of the Red Sea.

   How did God deliver the children of Israel from this situation? (Exodus 14:21-22)

   _____

   _____

   _____

5. By studying your map you will discover the Sinai peninsula is bordered by four bodies of water. What are these bodies of water called?

   North: _____ Sea

   South: _____ Sea

   West: Gulf of _____

   East: Gulf of _____

6. The "mountain of God," located in the high southern region of the Sinai Peninsula, is known today as Gebel Musa — the Mountain of Moses. It towers 7,497 feet above sea level and its summit is accessible only by a steep path leading up the virtually sheer rock cliff. The Bible calls this mountain by three different proper names. What are they?

   _____ (Exodus 3:1)

   _____ (Numbers 20:22)

   _____ (Exodus 19:20)

7. After receiving the law at Mt. Sinai, Moses and the children of Israel turned north, traveling through the desert to the location of the modern city of Elat at the northern terminus of the Gulf of Aqaba (or Gulf of Elat). Then they moved northwest to the oasis of Kadesh Barnea where spies were sent into Canaan to scout out the land.

   How long should it have taken the Israelites to travel from Mt. Sinai to Kadesh Barnea? (Deuteronomy 1:2)

   _____

8. When Moses was exiled into the Sinai the first time he stayed a total of 40 years, meaning he was 80 years old when he returned to Eygpt to lead the Hebrew slaves to freedom. However, instead of making the relatively short journey through the wilderness, the Hebrews — because of their grumbling and

NOTES

NOTES

rebellion — were required to remain in the Sinai until all the old generation had died off and a new generation had grown up. Moses, of course, remained with them as their leader that entire time.

How long was Moses in the wilderness the second time? (Numbers 14:33)

_____

MEMORY VERSE

Exodus 14:14 (Memorize, then write it on these lines)

_____

_____

Lesson 2
Purging: The Waters of Marah
The Importance of Starting Right

VIDEO REFERENCE: Lesson 2

The only way to achieve spiritual maturity is through the wilderness. Throughout the Bible we are reminded that for whatever reason we may find ourselves in the wilderness, God always uses these occasions for our purification and preparation.

An old Bible teacher used to remind his pupils that not only was the Lord interested in getting His people out of Egypt, He also wanted to get Egypt out of His people. That, perhaps, is the basic reason for all wilderness experiences. In the case of the Children of Israel this was not only symbolic — but practical. They had brought a great deal of Egypt with them (internally) as they entered the wilderness on their way to the promised land — which represents spiritual maturity.

Egypt was a filthy nation. The entire nation had recently undergone a siege of flies, locusts, dead frogs, boils and impure water. In the resulting plague, hundreds of thousands of Egyptian children had died. The Israelites, for the most part, had escaped the plagues. But they had brought with them the contaminations of Eygpt. These included not only amoebic dysentery, but *bilharzia*, a weakening disease borne by snails in the slow-moving irrigation ditches of the Nile Valley. (This condition still affects eighty percent of the peasants of Egypt.) These afflictions were known as "the diseases of Egypt."

Now, as we follow the Children of Israel from the shores of the *Yam Suf* (Sea of Reeds which is the northern extension of the Gulf of Suez which the Bible calls the Red Sea), they come to Marah. Here the Lord spoke to them and told them He would not allow the diseases of the Egyptians to afflict them — if they but obeyed Him.

Cleaning the System

The waters at Marah proved to be bitter. However, drinking the water would have brought almost instant purification since the water was filled with calcium and magnesium — a highly potent laxative. God's first stop for the Children of Israel was a potty stop.

Drinking the water, no matter how badly it tasted, would have brought almost instant purification. God was about to change the entire eating structure of the nation. He wanted these people to be a strong, healthy people. To accomplish this He began by purging their bodies — not only of the diseases they had brought with them, but in a spiritual sense to rid them of all their perverse yearnings and desires. In order to be truly "kosher" they not only had to refrain from pork, shellfish, and other gentile foods — they had to have a desire to be different, set apart, holy.

Strength for the Journey

There were additional reasons God brought the Israelites to Marah, of course. There always are. Calcium and magnesium form the basis of a drug called *dolomite*. Dolomite pills are used by professional athletes who perform in the sun. It is a muscle control drug to be used in extremely hot weather. It is sometimes used by patients with heart problems to control the heart muscle and keep it from going into fibrillation.

A Teaching Experience

The Israelites rebelled when confronted with God's plan. There was no room in their theology for a God who required hard things of people. They expected that of the master slaves of Eygpt — but they had been promised a land which flowed with milk and honey, not bitter waters which upset their stomachs and gave them diarrhea. The Bible says God *tested* the people at Marah. Testing in the Middle Eastern concept means to teach. A test is not a quiz to determine how much you've learned, but rather an experience designed by the teacher to share knowledge for the purpose of equipping you for the journey.

CONCLUSIONS

1. God's primary teaching at Marah was this: "If you cooperate with me, I will keep you healthy" (Exodus 15:26).

2. The journey to spiritual maturity must always begin with a desire to be holy.

3. Before you can receive God's best you must recognize that you are imperfect, that your life is basically unmanageable without God's control.

BIBLE STUDY

1. God's Guidance

The shortest route from Egypt (bondage to sin) to Canaan (spiritual maturity) is across the northern Sinai. Yet after leaving the *Yam Suf* (literal meaning Sea of Reeds which is the northern extremity of the Gulf of Suez — sometimes referred to in Exodus as the Red Sea), Moses turned south and led the Children of Israel into the wilderness.

It is important, from God's perspective, that each one of His followers have the same experience with Him that the leader has. God began by issuing instructions to Moses, but until each Israelite heard God individually, His best purpose could not be accomplished. Spiritual maturity is not for a select few — but for all.

Where did God tell Moses to bring the Children of Israel when they left Egypt? (Exodus 3:12)

_____

2. **God's Promise of Protection**

   Many Christians do not seek spiritual maturity because they fear the obstacles will be so great they might grow discouraged and return to the world of sin. They feel it is safer to remain as spiritual infants than to run the risk of combating Satan face to face — and losing. God is aware of this. If we allow Him to guide our footsteps He will keep us out of trouble.

   What might have happened to the Children of Israel if God had let them take the shortest route to Canaan? (Exodus 13:17)

   _____

   _____

   In the New Testament Paul enlarges on this concept, stating that God understands our weaknesses — especially when we are going through tough times.

   What will God do for us when we reach the limit of our ability to withstand temptation? (I Corinthians 10:13)

   _____

   _____

   When godly men have severe trials, what does God promise to do for them? (II Peter 2:9)

   _____

3. **We Must Desire Spiritual Maturity**

   Since *desire* is the key element needed to achieve spiritual maturity, God often leads us to places of desperation, forcing us to call out to Him for help. In the case of the Children of Israel, they had reached their utter limit of thirst before they found water.

   How many days did the Children of Israel travel in the desert without finding water? (Exodus 15:22)

   _____

4. **God's Purpose for Each of Us**

   God has a purpose for every action. When the Children of Israel arrived at the desert oasis they discovered the water was bitter — filled with minerals which they knew would ravage their intestinal systems. Rather than run the risk of vomiting and diarrhea, they refused to drink the water. Moses, who had been this way before, knew the water along the Gulf of Suez was laced with minerals. He also knew God had a purpose in wanting the Israelites to drink the bitter water. Despite their thirst, however, they refused to drink. It seemed they would rather die in the wilderness than suffer pain and inconvenience — which always accompanies growth into spiritual maturity. At that point God, understanding

NOTES

NOTES

their lack of spiritual commitment and inability to discern His will, allowed them to choose second best.

What two things did Moses do as a response to the grumbling of the Children of Israel? (Exodus 15:24-25)

(1.) _____

(2.) _____

5. Conditions for Health and Happiness

Following the people's failure to obey God and drink the bitter water, God laid down four important conditions. These conditions, which were to remain in force from then on (and are still the foundation stone for any permanent relationship of God) were given to show the people God was not a cruel God who forced His followers to drink water without reason. Instead, He is a loving and kind God who cares for us, who is concerned about our misery, and desires to heal all our diseases and keep us healthy. However, His *primary* purpose is not our health and happiness — but that we achieve spiritual maturity.

List the four things God commanded the Children of Israel to do in order to qualify for his healing touch. (Exodus 15:26)

(1.) _____
_____

(2.) _____
_____

(3.) _____
_____

(4.) _____
_____

God's love is absolute and His purposes are always fulfilled in us. Paul reminds us that the purpose of God for our lives is *predestined.*

For what purpose has God predestined us? (Romans 8:28-29)

_____
_____
_____

Jesus equated spiritual maturity with perfectness. In fact, in Matthew 5:48 the work "perfect" means "mature."

Who did Jesus say should be our model for spiritual maturity?
(Matthew 5:48)

_____

6. First Steps to Spiritual Maturity

Beginnings are of utmost importance. If you start a journey in the wrong direction it is impossible to reach your goal. A transcontinental airplane, off course by only one degree on the compass, will miss its intended destination by hundreds of miles. God wanted the Israelites to begin right — with clean systems. In the spiritual realm we clean our systems through a process called repentance. Repentance means a change of direction. It calls for deep self-inventory, admission of things wrong, and a resolve to move in the right direction by obeying God. It means you can never go back to Egypt.

When Peter spoke to those early Christians on the Day of Pentecost he called for a new direction for their lives. He said they should turn from their former ways, allow God to purge them of all the sin in their lives, set their faces toward a new goal. He said if they would do two things God would do two things which would give them power to continue on their journey toward spiritual maturity.

What are the two things Peter said God told the people they should do? (Acts 2:38)

(1.) _____

(2.) _____

What are the two things Peter said God would do if the people responded correctly? (Acts 2:38)

(1.) _____

(2.) _____

7. **The Journey to Spiritual Maturity Begins with Water Baptism**

   In I Corinthians 10:1-2 Paul refers to the journey of the Israelites as they left Egypt and equates that with water baptism. The Israelites were cut off from Egypt's slavery by passing through the Red Sea and the subsequent *engulfing* of Pharaoh's army by the water of the sea. They then moved on toward the promised land under the fiery pillar of cloud of God's supernatural presence.

   Paul also told the Christians in Rome, who had already been baptized in water, that the way would not be easy. He said there would be a tendency to want to "return to Egypt" (the bondage of sin) if they did not grasp the implications of their baptism.

   What does Paul say Water Baptism represents? (Romans 6:1-4)

   _____
   _____
   _____

8. **Baptism is the purging necessary to start the journey in the right direction.**

   Paul says water baptism (being "baptized unto His death") is the beginning of the journey to spiritual maturity. Through baptism you are purged of your old life — you leave beneath the baptismal waters all the sins of your past life (Egypt).

   What is the result of believing in Jesus Christ and following Him in Water Baptism? (Romans 6:22)

   _____

9. **Result of Cleansing**

   Purging, or cleansing, is for a purpose. It is not enough to simply be cleansed. God has an individual design for each of us.

NOTES

NOTES

Once we are cleansed we are then prepared to do what? (II Timothy 2:20-21)

_____
_____

10. Cleansed Through the Blood of Jesus

God's cleansing means we must not only accept Jesus as our Lord, but must be willing to take up His cross on a daily basis and follow Him (Matthew 10:38). That means we must die daily to the old way of life.

What does the Blood of Jesus Christ do so we may serve the Living God? (Hebrews 9:14)

_____
_____

WRAP UP

At first glance it seems that the only equipment required to begin our journey to spiritual maturity is obedience to a creed. This is not enough, however. The ancient Jews tried to follow the law God gave them, but were unable to do so. It is not enough to *believe*. Even Satan believes. Nor is it enough to *"believe and be baptized."* More is necessary and we will discuss that in the next lesson. The foundation, then, is not a creed (belief) or even an act (water baptism). Rather it is a person — the person of Jesus Christ. It begins with a *desire*, moves on to a *belief*, is followed by *act* and climaxes in becoming a *new person* when you are baptized in the Holy Spirit.

PERSONAL REVIEW QUESTIONS

1. T F God wants all His children to be healthy and happy.
2. T F The primary reason God wants us to obey Him is that we might be healthy and happy.
3. T F The journey to spiritual maturity should begin with **a desire** to become like Jesus.
4. T F God brought the Israelites to Marah to show them His miraculous power by changing the bitter water to sweet water.
5. T F When God "tested" the Israelites He was examining them to find out how much they had learned through the experience at the bitter water.
6. T F The word "Marah" actually means "miracle."
7. T F God gave the Israelites four conditions which, if met, would protect them from disease.
8. T F The New Testament teaches that belief in Christ and water baptism are essential if we are to move on to spiritual maturity.
9. T F Once we are baptized in water our problems are over.
10. T F Repentance means leaving the old ways behind and starting off in a new direction.
11. T F Pain and struggle are a part of the journey to spiritual maturity.
12. T F Baptism in water means we are leaving behind us the old life.

13. T F Taking up the **cross** of Jesus means a willingness to die to self desire on a daily basis.

14. T F Since Jesus "drank the bitter cup" by dying on Calvary, we no longer have to suffer or struggle with sin.

15. Have you brought some of the "diseases of the Egyptians" with you on your journey to spiritual maturity? In the margins of this book, or on a separate sheet of paper if you feel more comfortable, list the areas which need to be purged from your life.

MEMORY VERSE

Exodus 15:26 (Memorize, then write it on these lines.)

_____
_____
_____
_____

NOTES

TRUE OR FALSE ANSWERS

1-T, 2-F, 3-T, 4-F, 5-F, 6-F, 7-T, 8-T, 9-F, 10-T, 11-T, 12-T, 13-T, 14-F

Lesson 3
Provision: Filled with the Spirit
The Importance of Being Filled with the Holy Spirit

VIDEO REFERENCE: Lesson 3

For every Marah there is an Elim just beyond — a place of rest, refreshing, filling, and empowering for the rest of the journey.

The second stop on the journey to spiritual maturity, which begins with an emptying (repentance, baptism in water), is a place of filling — called by Jesus the baptism of the Holy Spirit. We find the parallel in the Old Testament story of the Children of Israel moving through the wilderness on their way to the Promised Land.

The Children of Israel, leaving the bitter water of Marah behind, moved on through the desert — still traveling south in an opposite direction from their final destination, until they arrived at a beautiful oasis called Elim. The place is described in the Bible as a lovely location with "twelve springs and seventy palm trees." Here the Israelites rested — and were strengthened for the journey ahead.

It was not enough for the Israelites to leave Egypt, to repent of all their old ways, even to be purged and delivered from all the remnants of the past. They needed a new kind of strength. The road ahead was to be a long road. In just a few days they would come face to face with a fearsome army of desert terrorists called Amalekites. The Israelites, at best a mob of former slaves, had never fought a battle. Indeed, it seems that few if any had ever stood up against an aggressor. They still had the mentality of slaves. Now God was equipping them — not only for the journey ahead — but to do battle with a powerful enemy who even then was lurking in the caves of Rephidim just ahead. The waters of Elim would give them strength.

Filled With the Holy Spirit

Many years later Jesus sat beside a well in Samaria and spoke to a Samaritan women about the power of God. He told her she needed more than water which would quench her physical thirst; she needed a "spring of water welling up to eternal life" (John 4:14). The woman recognized her spiritual thirst and pleaded with Jesus, "Sir, give me this water..." (John 4:15).

This is the same water Jesus spoke of later in the Gospel of John when He cried out to all who would listen to Him: "'If any man is thirsty, let him come to me and drink. Whoever believes in me, as the Scripture has said, streams of living water will flow from within him.' By this he meant the Spirit, whom those who believed in him were later to receive. Up to that time the Spirit had not been given, since Jesus had not yet been glorified" (John 7:37-39).

The journey to spiritual maturity is not all bitter water, even though it may begin with pain as most births do. The purpose for being emptied in repentance is so we may be filled with the Holy Spirit.

Without the presence and power of the Holy Spirit we cannot continue the journey — much less reach our destination which is being "conformed to the image of Jesus Christ" (Romans 8:29). Nor can we enjoy the journey. Without the Holy Spirit each step will be tortuous for it will be in our own strength. Not only that, the journey will be lonely — for we will not have the ability to gather friends around us. It will be dangerous, for we will not have the power to resist temptation or to drive away evil spirits. It will be powerless and boring, for we will not have the power to perform the exciting signs and wonders Jesus performed and desired His followers to perform.

Spiritual thirst afflicts all who move toward spiritual maturity. Our hope, however, lies in the words of Jesus: "Blessed are they which do hunger and thirst after righteousness: for they shall be filled" (Matthew 5:6).

In his concept of the "God-shaped vacuum," St. Augustine once confessed: "Our hearts are restless until we find our rest in Thee." That is the way it always is: spiritual thirst is the dominating factor in the lives of all humans. It begins with a deep longing for something to satisfy the inner cravings, and is fulfilled only when we are filled with the same Spirit who filled the Son of God and gave Him power to rise from the dead.

Sources of Water

In the wilderness there are three sources of water: rain water, which falls rarely and can be collected temporarily in cisterns hewed from rock; wells, which must be dug by hard labor and sometimes go dry; and springs — which flow continually. Jesus says the filling of the Holy Spirit is like a refreshing spring which gushes out of our "inner being," flowing continually regardless of the season, blessing us and blessing others.

Cisterns

As we examine our pilgrimage through the Christian life on our way to spiritual maturity it is easy to see how the sources of water in the desert parallel our spiritual resources also. Many people are receiving strength from collected water — rainwater which drains into cisterns. However, at best this is seasonal — available only when the rains come. Jeremiah warns of the dangers of depending on cistern water for strength — saying many cisterns leak and are unable to retain water (see Jeremiah 2:13).

Wells

Others spend their lives digging wells. Desert people often depend on wells for their water. They are dug by hand, the sides shored up with rocks and the sand pulled to the surface in buckets attached to long ropes. However, well water is often polluted or laced with minerals. Occasionally a sheep or a goat — or even a camel — will fall in a well and drown, ruining the water forever. Again we see the parallel as we

NOTES

watch Christians trying to achieve spiritual maturity in their own strength — by keeping the law, by performing good works, by attempting to overcome sin in their own strength. Not only is it impossible to achieve our goal in such a way, the Bible teaches, but those who try are never happy, never fulfilled, and never at peace with themselves and their brothers. It is a constant striving resulting in never reaching the goal.

Rivers of Living Water

Jesus intends for all Christians to be baptized, or immersed, in the Holy Spirit — just as He baptized His immediate followers on the Day of Pentecost. This experience leads us to the place where "rivers of living water" then flow from our most inner being. The fruit of the spirit as listed in Galatians 5:22-23 then become the norm for our behavior and attitude.

How May I Be Baptized in the Holy Spirit?

Being baptized in the Holy Spirit, then, is mandatory if you are to move on to spiritual maturity. How is this done? Jesus told His followers, following His resurrection and just before He ascended into Heaven, to go to an upper room and "wait for the gift my Father promised, which you have heard me speak about. For John baptized with water, but in a few days you will be baptized with the Holy Spirit" (Act 1:4-5).

Earlier, in His Sermon on the Mount, He had given instructions on how to receive the Holy Spirit. "Ask and it shall be given to you; seek and you will find; knock and the door will be opened to you... If you then, though you are evil, know how to give good gifts to your children, how much more will your Father in heaven give the Holy Spirit to those who ask Him" (Luke 11:9,13).

As you answer these questions, ask yourself these two questions: Have I been baptized in the Holy Spirit? If so, am I now filled with the Holy Spirit?

CONCLUSIONS

1. Before we can continue our journey to spiritual maturity we must receive power.

2. The power Jesus gives us is the power of the Holy Spirit.

3. Jesus desires that all His followers be filled with the Holy Spirit. The intial experience of this process is referred to in the Bible as the "baptism in the Holy Spirit" (Acts 1:5).

4. God's ultimate purpose for our lives is that we should be *conformed to the image of his Son*, Jesus Christ (Romans 8:29).

BIBLE STUDY

1. A Place of Filling and Refreshing

The Children of Israel left the bitter waters of Marah and moved south along the Gulf of Suez where they would eventually turn inland through a desert pass on their way to Mt. Sinai. It soon became evident they could not exist without water and refreshment. This was found at a place called Elim.

What is the Biblical description of Elim? (Exodus 15:27)

_____

_____

2. Going to the Proper Source

As we look at the water sources in the wilderness we see a parallel to the sources of spiritual power in our lives. What are the three basic sources of natural water in the desert? (Answers found at end of the chapter.)

_____, _____, _____

Cisterns

Cisterns are hewed from solid rock or dug in the hard ground in order to catch rainwater which runs off the mountains or from the roofs of houses. However, "runoff" water is never sufficient. It is there only in the rainy season. God says we must not depend on superficial surges of enthusiasm to keep us going. We need something far more lasting.

What were the two sins the prophet Jeremiah said the people had commited? (Jeremiah 2:13)

(1.) _____

_____

(2.) _____

_____

Wells

Others dig wells and depend on them to supply their water. While God honors those who work at their faith, He says that those who attempt to attain spiritual maturity by obeying the law — apart from being filled with the Spirit — are foolish.

Do we receive the Holy Spirit by obeying the law or by believing what God has said? (Galatians 3:2-3, 5) (Check the right answer.)

        Obeying _____

        Believing _____

Springs

Jesus indicates it is not enough to trap water in cisterns or to spend our time digging wells. What we need is a mighty flowing stream of water which will supply us with continual strength and power.

Where will that Living Water flow from? (John 7:37-38)

_____

To what was Jesus referring when he spoke of Living Water? (John 7:39)

_____

3. The Command of God

While Marah represents a place of emptying, the springs of Elim represent a place of filling, refreshing, empowering.

NOTES

NOTES

What kind of "filling" do we need if we are to complete our journey to spiritual maturity? (Ephesians 5:18)

_____

4. God's Ultimate Purpose for Our Lives

We need to remember that while it is mandatory that we be filled with the Holy Spirit, the experience of being "baptized in the Spirit" is not an end in itself. It is simply the means given us by God so we can attain an ever greater end.

What is God's ultimate purpose in our lives through the workings of the Holy Spirit? (Romans 8:29)

_____

_____

5. Satisfying Our Inner Yearnings

God understands our deepest spiritual needs. In fact, God put these needs in us, causing us to constantly yearn and search until we are fulfilled. This desire to be Christlike is at the root of all our yearnings. If we do not search for God we will, nevertheless, keep on searching — but in the wrong areas. It is only when we direct our search in the right area — seeking the fullness of the Holy Spirit — that we are at last satisfied and fulfilled.

What did Jesus say would happen to those who hunger and thirst after righteousness? (Matthew 5:6)

_____

6. The Beginning Step to Living a Life of Victory and Power

We learned in the previous chapter that baptism in water is a burial of the "old man." We now discover that baptism in the Spirit is an empowering of the "new man." The terminology was first introduced by John the Baptist when he referred to the ministry of Jesus.

What did John the Baptist say Jesus would do when He arrived? (Matthew 3:11)

_____

_____

Jesus told His disciples to wait — to refrain from ministry — until they had gone through this experience promised by John.

What did Jesus say would happen to His followers a few days afterward? (Acts 1:4-5)

_____

_____

This experience, Jesus said, would give His followers the needed power to continue their journey toward spiritual maturity.

What did Jesus tell His followers would happen to them as a result of the Baptism in the Holy Spirit? (Acts 1:8)

_____

_____

7. On the Day of Pentecost

Shortly after Jesus commanded His disciples to wait they were gathered in an upper room celebrating the Jewish Feast of Pentecost. In the Book of Acts Luke, the historian, points out the followers of Jesus — waiting on the promise that the risen Christ would return and baptize them in the Holy Spirit — had a powerful, life changing experience.

As we look at this from God's side we see the fulfillment of His promise. He has sent the Holy Spirit who had filled each follower of Jesus. From man's perspective we see two things which resulted from this mighty Spirit baptism.

What were these two things? (Acts 2:4)

(1.) _____

(2.) _____

It is not a case of either (1) or (2) but both. A true baptism in the Spirit means not only being full of the Holy Spirit but also overflowing in supernatural gifts. While speaking in tongues is not necessarily a sign of being baptized in the Spirit, nor is it necessarily the initial evidence of that experience, the Bible does teach that every Spirit baptized believer will exhibit some kind of supernatural gift as evidence of the filling of the Holy Spirit.

List the nine manifestations of the presence of the Holy Spirit as stated in I Corinthians 12:8-10.

(1.) _____

(2.) _____

(3.) _____

(4.) _____

(5.) _____

(6.) _____

(7.) _____

(8.) _____

(9.) _____

8. Speaking in Tongues

Although the Bible does not state that speaking in tongues always accompanies the baptism in the Holy Spirit, this particular gift, because of its uniqueness, does seem to be given primary status by the Holy Spirit. In most cases mentioned in the New Testament, speaking in tongues is not necessarily the *evidence* of the baptism in the Holy Spirit, it is the most frequent immediate *consequence*. Paul teaches that even though all may not speak in tongues, when the Holy Spirit is present in your life there is always a possiblity you will — for when He comes He brings ALL His gifts with Him, including this one.

While there are many reasons — most hidden to man — that the Holy Spirit gives the gift of speaking in other tongues to the Spirit baptized believer, here are five obvious ones.

1. It is the one gift God can use at will.

NOTES

NOTES

What are the two options the Spirit Baptized Christian has when he prays? (I Corinthians 14:14-15)

(1.) _____

(2.) _____

On the day of Pentecost, when the Christians were gathered in the upper room, Jesus returned and baptized them all in the Holy Spirit. However, those men and women then had to cooperate with the Spirit before the gift was manifested.

What did each of them do as an act of his own will? (Acts 2:4)

_____

2. It is the one new gift since Pentecost. All the other gifts seem to have been in operation prior to that time, although they were given only to special people at special times and were not for the entire body. For instance, Daniel was given the gift of interpretation of tongues when he interpreted four cryptic words written on a wall in the king's palace (Daniel 5:25-28). All the other gifts appeared at various times in Biblical history, but were not permanent — which is the basic difference between an *unction* and a *filling*.

3. The gift of tongues is basically a "prayer language," enabling us to pray to the Heavenly Father by direction of the Holy Spirit, rather than being directed by our own intellect. This means we can, be praying *in the Spirit,* pray for God's perfect will — because our prayer is directed by the Holy Spirit and not by our own intelligence or our own desires.

When we use the gift of speaking in tongues, to whom are we speaking? (I Corinthians 14:2)

_____

What is the Holy Spirit doing when we are praying in tongues? (Romans 8:26)

_____

_____

_____

4. Its use builds us up personally.

Who is helped and strengthened when we speak in tongues? (I Corinthians 14:4)

_____

5. On the Day of Pentecost a large number of unbelievers were attracted to the disciples. When they gathered Peter preached to them.

What attracted all those unbelievers to the disciples? (Acts 2:6)

_____

Unbelievers are always attracted to the supernatural. Tongues — like the performance of supernatural miracles — is one of God's finest tools for evangelism. Once the unbelievers are attracted, the Holy Spirit then uses other gifts, such as prophetic preaching, to convict them and show them the way of salvation.

For whom are tongues given as a sign? (I Corinthians 14:22)

_____

9. God wants all Christians filled with the Holy Spirit

Since the baptism in the Holy Spirit is a necessary step to equip us to move on to spiritual maturity, it is obvious God wants all of us filled with the Holy Spirit. Just as all those in the upper room on the Day of Pentecost were baptized in the Holy Spirit, so God wants all Christians today to have that same experience.

The promise of the Holy Spirit was not limited to those present at Pentecost but is for whom? (Acts 2:38-39)

_____

_____

10. How to Receive

What does Jesus promise to do when we are spiritually thirsty? (John 7:37-38)

_____

_____

_____

What are the three things we are to do to receive the Holy Spirit? (Luke 11:9-10)

(1.) _____

(2.) _____

(3.) _____

If we ask believing, what will the Heavenly Father give us? (Luke 11:13)

_____

Although the baptism in the Holy Spirit is often accompanied by great emotional release — i.e., weeping, laughing, physical shaking, speaking in tongues — there is a possibility none of these things may happen. However, since God always honors an honest and sincere prayer which is prayed in His will, and since it is His will to fill each Christian with His Holy Spirit, then despite the presence or absence of any kind of feeling or physical manifestation, we should accept God's gift by faith, praise Him for giving us the gift of the Holy Spirit, and immediately begin to walk in the Spirit.

PERSONAL REVIEW QUESTIONS

1. T   F   God wants all His followers to be baptized in the Holy Spirit.

2. T   F   Everyone who is filled with the Holy Spirit will receive supernatural power.

3. T   F   Speaking in tongues always accompanies the initial baptism in the Holy Spirit.

4. T   F   It is impossible to move on to spiritual maturity without the Holy Spirit.

5. T   F   All you need to do to be filled with the Holy Spirit is to sincerely ask God to fill you.

NOTES

NOTES

6. T   F   Speaking in tongues is the Holy Spirit speaking through you to God.

7. T   F   The various gifts of the Holy Spirit are reserved for just a few in the Body of Christ.

8. T   F   The ultimate purpose of God is that we might all speak in tongues.

9. T   F   Tongues is a sign to the unbeliever that God is present.

MEMORY VERSE

Acts 2:38 (Memorize, then write it on these lines)

_____

_____

_____

_____

TRUE OR FALSE ANSWERS

1-T, 2-T, 3-F, 4-T, 5-T, 6-T, 7-F, 8-F, 9-T.

ANSWERS TO QUESTION #2

(1) Cisterns, (2) Wells, (3) Springs.

Lesson 4
Obedience: Water from the Rock
Learning to Discern and Obey God's Voice

VIDEO REFERENCE: Lesson 4

There are two choices in life: doing things our way or doing things God's way. The Bible calls self-will *rebellion*. Living our lives in God's will is called *obedience*.

Obedience is the "road map" given to us to find our way through the maze of paths on our way to spiritual maturity.

Daring to Obey the Voice of God

Moses, leading the Children of Israel through the wilderness of the Sinai, turned inland through a great wadi, or canyon, through the mountains, and shortly arrived at a place where the water is near the surface of the earth — a place called Rephidim. Here God taught them another necessary lesson — the lesson of absolute obedience.

Once again they had used up all their water. As they had done earlier at Marah, they began to complain. Moses took a group of the tribal leaders and went ahead of the throng, up the wadi in the direction of Mt. Sinai — which towered ahead on the horizon. There he prayed, asking God what to do. Taking his staff he walked slowly, tapping the side of the rock canyon. He finally stopped. Moses knew that behind the rock, stored in a huge fissure or reservoir, was water which had been trapped during a previous deluge. As often happens, the water had forced its way into the huge fissure. Then, because of the high calcium content in the water, the small opening had closed up — sealed with calcium. In an action still used by the desert Bedouin called a *timile*, Moses drew back his staff and smashed the calcium covering. It broke and allowed the water to gush from the rock. There was enough to quench everyone's thirst.

Repeat Performance, Almost

Almost 40 years later, at a place called Kadesh Barnea in the northern Sinai, a similar incident occurred. Again, there was no water. This time, when Moses asked God what to do He received a slightly different answer. God told him to simply speak to the rock, not to strike it, commanding water to come forth. Instead Moses reverted to the old system: he struck the rock with this staff. It was a sad revelation of the fact Moses had become an old wineskin — no longer flexible and able to obey God as he had done earlier. His spirit, although faithful to God, had lost its elasticity. He no longer had the willingness to expand. It was easier to do it as he had done in the past than to venture out and attempt something new, even though God had commanded it.

As a result of Moses' disobedience — which was basically an unwillingness to do things God's new way — God removed Moses from leadership and forbad him from entering Canaan with the rest of the people.

God Judges Those Who Deliberately Disobey Him

As we journey toward spiritual maturity one of the lessons we must learn is the lesson of obedience. God knows that ultimate happiness comes only when we walk in His Will as obedient children. No man, no leader, is indispensible. As we study the life of Moses we discover that God wants leaders who can take orders from Him without question or reservation. God equates disobedience with rebellion which He says is like witchcraft — or the worship of Satan. It is a serious charge. In fact, when Jesus talked about willful disobedience, He did it in the context of God acting as a final judge who banishes the disobedient ones into hell (Matthew 7:21-22).

One of the gifts of the Holy Spirit which comes when we are filled with the Holy Spirit is the ability to "discern spirits" — that is, to distinguish the voice of God from the many other voices we hear along the road to spiritual maturity. The Holy Spirit, then, gives us the ability to hear God. Our task is to obey that voice as He speaks to us about all things great and small.

CONCLUSIONS

1. What worked yesterday is not sufficient for today.

2. God's direction yesterday must be made fresh by His word today.

3. To be tyrannized by the past is the worst of all tyrannies.

4. The rut of tradition is but one step removed from a grave in the wilderness.

5. God's word to each of us is fresh every morning.

6. The man who trusts in God will never be embarrassed or defeated.

BIBLE STUDY

1. **Obedience Commanded**

    God does not make suggestions. He commands. He does not say, "Why don't you?", He says "Do this" and "Don't do that." The commands of God are plain, simple, and are not grievous. They are not difficult to keep and they always bring happiness. The human will, however, which is in rebellion, does not want to take orders from God. We prefer to obey when it is convenient, and do it our way the rest of the time. God, then, is continually chastising us — as a parent corrects a child — to bring us to the place of obedience. If we persist in disobeying He will not force us, but will leave us to our own devices which ultimately bring us to ruin, heartache, and eventual death.

On the other hand, if we obey God's commands we are blessed above all people.

What did God promise Moses if the Israelites obeyed Him and kept His covenants? (Exodus 19:5-6)

_____

_____

_____

2. Obeying God's Messengers

There is a tendency to say, "Well, when I hear God speak I'll obey Him." However, the Bible says the voice of God comes in many ways. It comes through His written word — the Bible. It comes through His servants as they prophesy. It comes through the priests and pastors who lead the flock. It comes through those in godly authority over us. To wives it comes through a godly husband. To children it comes through godly parents. It may come to parents through godly children, or to husbands through godly wives. It may come through a friend exercising the "word of wisdom" or the gift of "prophecy." On at least one occasion God spoke to Moses through an angel — commanding Moses to obey him.

What did God say He would do if Moses obeyed the angel of the Lord? (Exodus 23:20-22)

_____

_____

3. Risking Failure by Obeying

Even though Moses was a wise student of the desert and knew that water was often obtained by bashing the rock with his staff in the proper place, nevertheless there was always the chance he might strike the rock at the wrong place, or that the water behind the rock might have seeped into the ground and was no longer there. To obey God, then, was risky, for it meant Moses might lose face in the eyes of the tribal leaders if he failed. Moses, however, chose to obey God, believing it was better to obey and fail, than to disobey and lose God's blessing.

When God gave Moses the command to strike the rock He also gave him a promise. What did God promise Moses He would do if Moses obeyed? (Exodus 17:5-6)

_____

_____

4. Promise of Reward

Although we do not obey God in order to be rewarded (rather we obey Him because He is God and there is no other option), God is faithful to reward those who do obey Him. He awards them by "blessing" them. Blessing means to make happy. When we bless God we make Him happy. When God blesses us He makes us happy. In a series of beatitudes at the beginning of His Sermon on the Mount, Jesus used the word "blessed" a number of times, saying certain people (such as the meek, those who hunger and thirst for righteousness, the peacemakers, the pure in heart, etc.) are blessed — or made happy by God (Matthew 5:3-11). Therefore, it is proper to expect God to bless you when you obey.

NOTES

The writer of Hebrews points out a particular characteristic of God which separates Him from humans. What is it? (Hebrews 6:10)

_____

_____

What happens to the man whose desire is to obey God in all matters? (James 1:25)

_____

_____

5. **Penalties of Disobedience**

   Although we are under the grace of God, and our God is a god of forgiveness whose infinite loving-kindness covers all our sins, Jesus says that God treats harshly those — even those who say they are His followers — who deliberately and willfully disobey His commands. In fact there is serious ground to believe that God banishes from His presence those who willfully disobey.

   What did Jesus say was more important than calling God Lord with your lips? (Matthew 7:21)

   _____

   _____

   Jesus says God is extremely harsh on those who choose to indulge their own selfish desires rather than doing the will of God.

   What does Jesus say He will tell those — in the final judgment — who call God "Lord" but continue to live lives of disobedience? (Matthew 7:23)

   _____

   _____

6. **Even God's Choice Servants Suffer When They Disobey**

   No man in history was more obedient to God than Moses. Yet at the end of his life, Moses willfully and deliberately disobeyed God. In this case, God wanted to glorify Himself through the situation, but instead Moses stepped forward and took the glory. God does not share His glory with any man, even His choicest servants. As a result Moses was disqualified for leadership, was prevented from accompanying the Israelites into the Promised Land, and died alone in the wilderness while the others went on ahead.

   In your own words describe what took place at Kadesh Barnea. (Numbers 20:6-11)

   _____

   _____

   _____

   _____

   What was different in God's command to Moses in Exodus 17:6 and His command in Numbers 20:8?

   _____

   _____

What did God say would happen to Moses and Aaron since they disobeyed? (Numbers 20:12)

_____

_____

7. God's Standard for His Leaders

Jesus said that unto whom much is given, much is required. God expects more of those who lead than He does of those who merely follow. All are required to obey and all are blessed with the same blessing when they do obey. However, God's expectations for His leaders are even higher.

How will leaders be judged by God? (James 3:1)

_____

8. God's Highest for Mankind

Many years after Moses had passed from the scene God spoke through an old prophet, Samuel. God had given King Saul some specific directions, just as He had given directions to Moses about speaking to the rock. King Saul had disobeyed God but then tried to make up for it by offering sacrifices — even giving God some of the goods he had stolen as an offering.

What did Samuel tell Saul about God's expectations? (I Samuel 15:22)

_____

_____

_____

Samuel went ahead to warn King Saul about the seriousness of his disobedience.

To what does God compare the sin of willful disobedience? (I Samuel 15:23)

_____

_____

What was the result of King Saul's disobedience? (I Samuel 15:23)

_____

_____

9. The Results of Disobedience

Throughout the Bible the prophets as well as the writers of the New Testament keep referring to the disobedience of the Children of Israel as they wandered through the wilderness. The prophet Isaiah says the Israelites actually "grieved the Holy Spirit" by their disobedience.

What did God do when His children grieved the Holy Spirit?
(Isaiah 63:10)

_____

_____

_____

_____

NOTES

Where does God say those who willfully disobey Him will spend the rest of their days? (Psalm 68:6)

_____

10. **Learning to Obey**

    Obedience, like all traits, is a habit. It must be learned. We teach our children to obey by spanking their hands if they are about to touch a hot stove. Animal trainers teach dogs to obey by switching their legs and then offering rewards when they do what is right. Fish trainers have taught dolphins, even whales, to do tricks by giving them fish as a reward.

    How did Jesus learn to obey His Heavenly Father? (Hebrews 5:8)

    _____

11. **Disobedience Puts Us In Bondage**

    The purpose of obeying God is that we might be set free from the thing which enslaves us. The Bible says sin binds us. Obedience sets us free.

    What is the final result of bondage to sin? (Romans 6:16)

    _____

    What is the final result of being a slave to obedience? (Romans 6:16)

    _____

12. **God's Wonderful Promise**

    Despite all the warnings of God's wrath on those who disobey Him, He understands our weakness and looks upon our hearts to judge us, rather than upon our actions. When God brought the Israelites out of Egypt He did not just give them commands and warnings, He also gave them a wonderful promise.

    What was God's promise to those who obeyed Him? (Jeremiah 7:23)

    _____
    _____
    _____

13. On this paper, or on a separate sheet if you desire for privacy's sake, list the areas of your life where you know you are being disobedient to God.

    _____
    _____
    _____
    _____
    _____
    _____
    _____
    _____
    _____

PERSONAL REVIEW QUESTIONS

1. T F There are two choices in life: do things God's way or do things our way.
2. T F Sometimes God gives commands, sometimes He makes suggestions.
3. T F God told Moses if he would strike the rock at Rephidim He would "go before him."
4. T F God told Moses the same thing at Kadesh Barnea.
5. T F Although Moses disobeyed God at Kadesh Barnea, since Moses had led a godly life for 120 years God did not hold him accountable.
6. T F God severely punished Moses for disobeying Him.
7. T F Ultimate happiness comes only when we walk in God's will for our lives.
8. T F God wants leaders who give Him absolute obedience.
9. T F God judges His leaders with a different standard than those who merely follow.
10. T F God says willful disobedience is like witchcraft.
11. T F Jesus says those who willfully disobey God will be banished to outer darkness.
12. T F When the Children of Israel disobeyed they grieved the Holy Spirit.
13. T F Although God desires our sacrifices, He prefers our obedience.
14. T F Obedience to God can be learned.
15. T F Jesus did not have to learn obedience since He was God.

MEMORY VERSE

I Samuel 15:22 (Memorize, then write it on these lines.)

_____
_____
_____

TRUE OR FALSE ANSWERS

1-T, 2-F, 3-T, 4-F, 5-F, 6-T, 7-T, 8-T, 9-T, 10-T, 11-T, 12-T, 13-T, 14-T, 15-F

Lesson 5
Authority: Coming into Submission
God's Government

VIDEO REFERENCE: Lesson 5

The original government of the Hebrew people was patriarchal. The head of the family — the patriarch — exercised supreme rule over all his descendants. His married sons did the same with their children and other descendants while still remaining submissive to the supreme head of the tribe, or family. At the father's death his firstborn succeeded him in supreme headship. Since only men of mature age came into these positions, they became known as "elders," the term meaning, literally, one with a grey beard.

When the Hebrews journeyed into Egypt, four hundred years before the time of Moses, their patriarch was a man by the name of Jacob (now called Israel) who was the son of another patriarch, Isaac, who had been the son of the original tribal leader, Abraham. Although the children of Jacob became leaders of 12 separate tribes, or clans, the entire group was still known as the Children of Israel — or Israelites. It was this group of people who were forced into slavery in Egypt and were eventually set free under the leadership of Moses, who came from the tribe of Levi.

Moses: A Man Under Authority

When God commissioned Moses and sent him back to Egypt to lead the freedom march toward the Promised Land, he said the first thing he should do on returning to Egypt was contact the old tribal elders. What a strange command, for these old men had no earthly authority. They were but mere echoes of a long forgotten government. They served in form only and were just as much slaves to the Egyptians as any of the others. Yet God specifically told Moses to go to these elders, submit to them, and enlist their help in confronting Pharaoh.

God had a reason for this. First, He knew Moses needed men to stand with him when he confronted Pharaoh. He also knew that Moses was fallible, prone to mistakes in judgment and action. The combined wisdom of these men would be necessary if Moses were to hear God correctly. Finally, God's intent with the people of Israel was not just to set them free but to place them under government.

Once they had been slaves. Now he was going to teach them that He, God, was a god of authority and submission. If they were going to become like Him, they needed to learn to take authority and to submit to authority. Therefore, it was God's intent to reestablish the people of Israel under godly government — the government of elders.

Forming An Army

As the Israelites moved deeper into the Sinai, it became evident that without submission to leadership they would be lost. No place was this clearer than when the group arrived at Rephidim and were attacked by the fierce army of Amalek — a band of cave-dwelling terrorists. According to Genesis 36:12, Amalek was a grandchild of Esau — Jacob's brother. Their hatred for their distant cousins had increased across the years. Not only did they not fear their Jewish cousins, they did not even fear God (Deuteronomy 25:18).

Moses knew the battle with the Amalekites was more than a skirmish with desert bandits. The Amalekites were the forerunners of all these nations who even today are determined to wipe out God's people. They attacked the old people, the children, the pregnant women and the sick — those who were lagging behind the main group as they trudged through the desert. They were genuine terrorists, maiming, plundering, and slaughtering. Moses had no choice but to deal with them.

Until this point in history, Moses had been both leader and overseer, pastor and apostle, prophet and priest. At Rephidim his role as leader began to change. He was now 81 years old and, although still healthy and strong, realized the call on his life had changed from that of line officer to that of field general. It was time to exert his authority, not only as physical leader, but as the spiritual head of the people.

Delegated Authority

He began by appointing Joshua, a loyal young warrior, as his second-in-command. He commissioned him to select his own men to fight with him. Moses then climbed to the top of a small mountain overlooking the valley. His brother, Aaron, and his brother-in-law, Hur, went with him. Moses raised his staff over the valley. It was the signal Joshua had waited for. He attacked. Moses knew he was doing more than directing the fight from his mountain vantage point: he was interceding — standing between the people and God as their high priest. When his arms grew tired and he lowered the staff, the battle went against the Israelites. As long as he asserted his authority — shown by the uplifted staff — the battle went for the Israelites. Seeing this, Aaron and Hur stepped forward and supported their leader — submitting to him by lifting up his arms until the battle was over.

This visual lesson of Moses' authority, of the delegated authority of Joshua, of the submission of secondary leaders to the primary leader, and the submission of the people to all leadership, remains the principle of God's government in the church today. At no time in history did God call a committee to do His work. He chooses men — elders — and gives those men authority. He expects them to take authority over others. He calls on His people to submit to leaders — both spiritual leaders and governmental leaders.

The Kingdom of God is not a democracy — with a one-man, one-vote rule. It is a theocracy. God is in charge. He appoints leaders to carry out His orders. He expects His people to submit to those leaders by holding up their hands and carrying out their orders. In a nation like the USA, founded on rebellion and fiercely proud of our independence, this is not a popular concept. But the church of Jesus Christ is not mandated by the Constitution, it is directed by the Bible. Submission to authority is necessary if we are to attain spiritual maturity.

NOTES

CONCLUSIONS

1. God calls men to carry out His will on earth.
2. God delegates authority to men and we are to submit to those whom God has set over us in leadership.

BIBLE STUDY

1. Moses Under Authority

When Moses returned to Egypt to confront Pharaoh, he did not go immediately to the palace. Instead, he returned to the ghetto where the Israelites lived.

Why did Moses go first to the Israelites rather than going directly to Pharaoh? (Exodus 3:18, 4:29-31)

_____
_____
_____

As the Israelites were preparing to enter the Promised Land, many years later, Moses began to organize the people under proper spiritual leadership. Although they were to continue to be submissive to their new leader, Joshua, they would also have other authorities over them.

What did God tell Moses to do and what would be the result of his action? (Numbers 11:16-17)

_____
_____
_____
_____

2. Jesus and Submission

The first 30 years of the life of Jesus were spent in preparation for His ministry. During these years He was in submission to His parents, to earthly authority, and to His religious overseers. During this time of submission He grew into spiritual maturity.

What was Jesus' relationship with His earthly parents? (Luke 2:51)

_____

What was the result of His submission? (Luke 2:52)

_____
_____
_____

Even though Jesus knew He was God's Son, He submitted Himself to those God had placed in authority over His life. No matter how much knowledge we gain, God has us in relationship with others that they may help, encourage, and give balance to our lives.

3. Jesus Respects Authority and Submission

Shortly after Jesus began His public ministry, a Roman centurion, a commander of 100 men, came to Him asking for help. The officer's servant was at home dying. The Roman soldier asked Jesus for help. When Jesus said He would come to the man's house, the soldier said that was not necessary.

How did the man's answer let Jesus know he understood authority and submission? (Matthew 8:5-10)

_____

_____

_____

4. Areas Where God's People Are To Submit

(1) Family

There is a God-given structure for the family outlined in the Scripture. The husband (father) is to give loving leadership and provision to his wife and children. He is to be the priest in his home, interceding for his flock. He is the pastor to his wife and children, giving them spiritual care and direction.

How should a husband love his wife? (Ephesians 5:25, 28)

_____

_____

The wife is to live in a relationship of love and submission to her husband.

How is a wife to submit to her husband? (Ephesians 5:22-24)

_____

_____

_____

Children are to be in a submitted relationship also.

What is God's command for children? (Colossians 3:20)

_____

_____

How should a father take authority over his child? (Colossians 3:21)

_____

_____

How should a father discipline his child? (Proverbs 13:24)

_____

_____

What are the two things God says children should do for their parents? (Ephesians 6:1-2)

(1) _____

(2) _____

NOTES

(2) Relationships With Each Other

The Bible is strong in its teaching that if we are to move on to spiritual maturity we must do so by submitting to authority. Especially is this true in the sometimes sticky areas of life. Although we no longer have slavery, the principle of a slave's relationship with his master still applies in our relationship with our employer or supervisor on the job.

How should a slave react to an unjust master? (I Peter 2:18)

_____

_____

What special instruction does God give on how younger people should relate to older people? (I Peter 5:5)

_____

(3) Human Government

The Lord instructs us to submit to the laws decided upon by human government and courts of law. Governments are ordained by God to keep order, punish evildoers, and reward the good.

To whom does God tell us to submit? (I Peter 2:13-14)

_____

_____

What does God say about our relationship to government rulers? (Romans 13:1-5)

_____

_____

_____

(4) Church Leaders

God has ordained elders, or leaders, in the church. He tells us to submit to them. In so doing we remain under God's protection.

Why should we obey spiritual leaders? (Hebrews 13:17)

_____

_____

How should we react to elders in the church? (I Timothy 5:1, 19)

_____

_____

By submitting to the elders of the church we should expect certain benefits.

What in particular can we expect if we let the elders minister to us in time of need? (James 5:14, 15)

_____

_____

5. Exception to the Rule

In true Biblical submission we are submitting "as unto Christ." For that reason a wife can submit to an ungodly husband, a child to an ungodly parent, an employee to an ungodly supervisor — and do it "unto the Lord." Actually what we are doing is submitting to the authority God has placed in them. The wife, then, is actually submitting to the office of the husband, the employee to the office of employer, the citizen to the office of governor or policeman. However, once that individual usurps God's authority, there is another principle which applies. There is a time to refuse (not rebel). Daniel refused a direct order of the king to worship a false God. The disciples refused to stop preaching about Jesus, even when commanded to do so by religious authorities. Even though they all *respected* the office of those in authority, they chose to suffer the consequences rather than disobey God.

What did Peter and John tell the religious leaders when commanded to stop preaching? (Acts 5:29)

_____

_____

_____

PERSONAL REVIEW QUESTIONS

1. T F God wanted the Israelites to set up a democratic society, but because they grumbled He appointed Moses over them as leader.
2. T F The Amalekites would have run from the Children of Israel, but Joshua insisted on picking a fight with them.
3. T F One of the first things God did with the Israelites was to establish government.
4. T F When the Israelites finally entered the Promised Land, God let them have their one-man, one-vote rule.
5. T F The elders were the leaders of the tribes.
6. T F Elder literally means one with a grey beard.
7. T F God blesses men and women who are not afraid to submit to authority.
8. T F We are to submit to good government leaders, but rebel against evil leaders.
9. T F God still places elders in the church.
10. T F Peter told the slaves of the day to run away and obtain their freedom.
11. T F Jesus rebuked the Roman centurion because he submitted to a heathen government.
12. T F We are to submit to elders in the church as long as we agree with them.

TRUE OR FALSE ANSWERS

1-F, 2-F, 3-T, 4-F, 5-T, 6-T, 7-T, 8-F, 9-T, 10-F, 11-F, 12-F

NOTES

MEMORY VERSE

Ephesians 5:21 (Memorize, then write it on these lines.)

_____

_____

_____

Lesson 6
Changed Appetites: Manna from Heaven
Making All Things New

VIDEO REFERENCE: Lesson 6

God has placed within us certain drives, or appetites. These are basic instincts which are neither moral nor immoral. They are the driving forces of our lives:

(1) The need for security.
(2) The need for recognition.
(3) The need for love — to love and to be loved.
(4) The need for adventure.
(5) The need to create.

These drives (appetites), either by themselves or working in combination, control most of our life patterns.

Our problems come not because we have these appetites, but because of where we go to be fed. Instead of coming to God to have our needs met, we go to the wrong source. "My people have committed two sins," God told Jeremiah, "They have forsaken me, the spring of living water, and have dug their own cisterns, broken cisterns that cannot hold water" (Jeremiah 2:13).

God does not want to kill our appetites. He simply wants us to drink from His well and eat from His table.

Eating From God's Table

The need for *security* is to be met through a secure relationship with God which eliminates all fear.

The need for *recognition* is met through the realization of our status before God as a royal priest, as a joint heir with Jesus Christ, as a "son of God."

The need for *love* — to love and to be loved — is met by our love relationship with Jesus Christ and by being part of a loving family called the church, which is the "body of Christ" on earth.

The need to be *adventurous* does not have to be met by reckless lifestyle but is satisfied by walking in faith.

NOTES

The final appetite, the need to *create*, means we are like God Himself who is the Creator. By allowing Him to re-form us in the image of His Son, we are not only given the ability to create wonderful things, but we literally become new creatures ourselves. Thus all our appetites are satisfied when we eat at God's table.

Called To Be Different

We see this when we examine God's way of dealing with the Israelites in the wilderness. God's intent for these former slaves was to turn them into a nation of priests — people who would not only represent Him throughout all history, but would reflect Him as well. He had "chosen" them as a race of people set apart — a people who would be a light to all other people in the world. They would be "holy" (the word literally means "set apart"), different. They would not be like other people who behave like animals — they would be a people under discipline, a people who take their orders from a different source, a people whose needs and appetites are met by God — not by selfish indulgence.

In order to accomplish this, God first had to cleanse their systems of all the old things — both the old appetites and the old diseases. That was the purpose for having them stop at Marah. Then He filled them with a new spirit. This should have resulted in a grateful people who would be eager to take all God offered. The next step was to reveal His ability to provide for them when they had nothing. He was teaching them to believe in Him. So, when their water ran out He gave them water from a rock. When their food ran out He literally gave them food from heaven. It was called *manna* and was described as "white like coriander seed and tasted like wafers made with honey" (Exodus 16:31). Moses called it "bread" and told the people to gather it and eat it. It was God's provision since their food had run out. It would last them until they reached the Promised Land, just a few miles to the north.

God's Original Plan

We need to remember it was not God's original plan for the Israelites to have to eat manna for 40 years. His original plan was for them to learn His ways and move as quickly as possible out of the wilderness into the Promised Land which "flowed with milk and honey" — a land that typifies "spiritual maturity." However, the people balked. They yearned for the old way of life. They grumbled at God's provision of manna, constantly wishing they were back in Egypt eating the old diet. Therefore God had no choice but to leave them in the wilderness until their appetites changed — for He was determined to raise up a group of people who were holy, who did not yearn for fleshly things but yearned for spiritual maturity instead. His desire was — and is — to have followers who delight to do His will.

Of course, in reading the Bible we discover the people did not cooperate with God, and thus God's measures were much more harsh and stern than they would have been had the people submitted. In fact, they had to remain in the desert until the entire older generation died and a new generation — people with changed appetites — grew up. Yet His best plan for them was to show His loving-kindness and His mercy even as He changed them.

God had another reason for the manna than merely to reveal His ability to provide for them. It was to make the change easier as He transformed their entire appetite system. At Mt. Sinai, God literally changed the diet of the Israelites. He told them that one of the outward signs of their holiness was the fact they would never again eat like other people. This would set them apart as different. Certain foods would be forbidden. (Incidentally, those foods which God forbad the Israelites to eat have since been questioned by many medical and nutrition authorities to be unhealthy.) Those foods which were allowed were to be prepared in special ways. The diet would be called *kosher*. It was a diet which would remain in effect until Jesus fulfilled the Law and God revealed — in the new covenant with His people — that real holiness was not determined by keeping dietary laws, but by an attitude of the heart.

CONCLUSIONS

1. God has a purpose for everything He does.
2. In order to become the kind of people God wants us to be, we must be willing to change our appetites.
3. Grumbling over God's diet is a sure way to get more of the same.
4. God will supply all our needs.

BIBLE STUDY

1. God's Provision

Despite the fact manna was God's provision, it was quite bland. The Israelite women used great ingenuity to change its appearance — but manna was a radical change of diet for people who had grown accustomed to the spices and meats of Egypt. The first encounter with manna came when the Israelites ran out of food after leaving Elim on their way to Mt. Sinai. It was another remarkable evidence of God's care and His ability to provide.

What did Moses call this strange stuff which fell from heaven? (Exodus 16:15)

_____

_____

Moses gave specific instructions as to how the manna was to be gathered. When the instructions were not followed, the manna spoiled.

What were Moses' instructions? (Exodus 16:16-26)

_____

_____

_____

_____

Describe the manna. (Exodus 16:31)

_____

_____

2. The People's Response

The Israelites complained about the manna, as they complained about every-

NOTES

NOTES

thing. The tragedy of human history is that man never seems to learn from his mistakes, or the mistakes of those who have gone before him. The man who insists on learning everything from personal experience seldom makes any progress. We see this in Paul's letter to the church at Corinth when he has to warn them not to repeat history by having the same attitude as the Children of Israel who grumbled over God's provision.

What are the five things Paul says displease God? (I Corinthians 10:6-10)

(1) _____
(2) _____
(3) _____
(4) _____
(5) _____

God was trying to woo the people away from their former love of self-indulgence to a place of depending upon Him to satisfy all their appetites. They were too shortsighted to understand a God who insisted on closing the door to Egypt's food forever, and who was more interested in teaching them the discipline of obedience than in satisfying their carnal cravings.

Temptation — the desire to return to the appetites of Egypt — demands a tempter, one who stimulates our minds away from God.

Who were the tempters among the Israelites? (Numbers 11:4-6)

_____

3. Our Relationship With Unbelievers

Many of the laws given from Mt. Sinai dealt with mixing with unbelievers. The people who kept stirring up the Israelites by crying to go back to Egypt were described by the Bible as the "rabble," or the "mixed multitude." These were the Egyptians who accompanied the Israelites on their exodus to the Promised Land. They were constantly provoking the Israelites to renounce God and return to Egypt. Jesus later pointed out that no man can serve two masters, and Paul talked about those "enemies of the cross."

How did Paul describe those who try to entice us away from God?
(Philippians 3:18-19)

_____

_____

_____

What does God's Word tell us to do in relationship with unbelievers?
(II Corinthians 6:17)

_____

_____

4. Different Appetites

God contrasts the diet of Egypt with His new diet. The diet of Egypt was pleasing. The new diet was healthy. It's not that the new food did not taste good — for taste is relative. What we like to eat depends on our culture. The new diet commanded by God was different and the people rejected change. God is changeless. Yet, for us to become like Him and move into spiritual maturity we must change. That is where the conflict comes — between God's commands and our desires.

What does Malachi teach us about the nature of God? (Malachi 3:6)

_____

In order to change into His likeness, certain steps are necessary. We see this in the march of the Israelites. They had to leave Egypt, be purged of their old desires, be filled with a new spirit, then start on a new diet.

How does Paul outline these spiritual steps when he talks about moving on to spiritual maturity? (Ephesians 4:22-24)

_____

_____

_____

What did Paul say we should take off and what should we put on? (Colossians 3:9-10)

_____

_____

5. Wrong Desires

The book of Proverbs often contrasts the appetites of the godly man with the appetites of the sinful man. The sinful man wants that which brings him pleasure. The godly man wants that which God wants him to have.

What does Proverbs have to say about our desire for riches? (Proverbs 23:4-5)

_____

_____

Jesus also warned us about our often consuming appetite to make money.

What did Jesus say about this in Matthew 6:24?

_____

_____

What did Jesus tell us to do about our desire to store up riches for personal gain? (Matthew 6:19-21)

_____

_____

6. Singing A New Song

The Bible has much to say about newness. David says in Psalm 40:3 that we are to sing a new song. God told Isaiah that he was making all things new (Isaiah 43:19).

NOTES

What does the Bible have to say about the mercies of God? (Lamentations 3:23)

_____

_____

Jesus said He was giving us a "new commandment" which would reflect our changed appetites.

What is the new commandment Jesus gave us? (John 13:34)

_____

_____

If we practice Jesus' new commandment what will be the result? (John 13:35)

_____

_____

This newness the Bible talks about is a result of our changed appetites — our desire to seek after godly things. The man who has been "raised with Christ" is told to do certain things.

What should be the direction of our new appetites? (Colossians 3:1-2)

_____

_____

7. The New Covenant

One of the new things the Bible speaks of is a New Covenant between God and man. The Old Covenant was given to Moses on Mt. Sinai and then passed along to the people. It had to do with the Law. The people were commanded to keep the Law of God. If they did, God would bless and protect them. Jesus came to bring us a New Covenant. But long before He appeared, the prophets told us what would happen.

What did Jeremiah say God would do when the Messiah appeared? (Jeremiah 31:31)

_____

_____

What was to be the difference between the Old Covenant and the New Covenant? (Jeremiah 31:32-33)

_____

_____

_____

What would be the result of this New Covenant? (Jeremiah 31:34)

_____

_____

What has God done for us under this New Covenant? (II Corinithians 3:6)

_____

_____

Jesus referred to this New Covenant a number of times. In fact, He said He Himself was the New Covenant. The night before He died on the cross He told His disciples that His shed blood was the blood of the New Covenant, just as the shed blood of the sacrificial lamb was the blood of the Old Covenant.

How did Jesus tell us to remember His sacrifice? (I Corinithians 11:23-26)

_____

_____

_____

What does Paul say we are transformed into? (II Corinthians 3:18)

_____

_____

PERSONAL REVIEW QUESTIONS

1. T F God punished the Israelites for their grumbling by making them eat manna.
2. T F Since the Israelites refused to drink the bitter water at Marah, God told them they could never again taste pork or eat shellfish.
3. T F Those driving forces in each of us need to be killed before God can use us effectively.
4. T F God told the Israelites they were to be a holy people.
5. T F Holiness is shown by the clothes we wear and the way we style our hair.
6. T F Holiness means to be different, or "set apart," from the world.
7. T F The Israelites were chosen to be a light to the Gentiles. That means they were to reveal God to them — especially through the Messiah.
8. T F God did not originally intend for the Israelites to eat manna for 40 years.
9. T F God left the Israelites in the desert for 40 years because the women insisted on cutting their hair short like the men.
10. T F When Paul said we were to be new creatures, he meant our appetites should change and we should desire to do things God's way rather than our way.
11. T F Jesus said the Lord's Supper should remind us of His sacrifice on the cross.
12. T F The "new commandment" which Jesus gave us means we no longer have to obey God.
13. T F God's New Covenant with mankind was fulfilled in Jesus.

NOTES

14. T F Paul includes grumbling against God in the same group of evils as sexual immorality.

15. T F Once the Israelites stopped their grumbling, God allowed some of them to return to Egypt for occasional visits.

MEMORY VERSE
II Corinthians 5:17 (Memorize, then write it on these lines)

_____

_____

_____

TRUE OR FALSE ANSWERS

1-F, 2-F, 3-F, 4-T, 5-F, 6-T, 7-T, 8-T, 9-F, 10-T, 11-T, 12-F, 13-T, 14-T, 15-F

Lesson 7
Restoration: Spiritual Dominion
Taking Authority in God's Name

VIDEO REFERENCE: Lesson 7

Throughout history it is clear that God's ultimate destiny for man is to rule with His Son. This was God's intent when He created man and woman. He placed them in the Garden of Eden and gave them dominion over every living thing. However, Adam sinned, and because of his sin — which was basically choosing to do things his way rather than God's way — he lost his ability to reign over this earth. From that time on, man was at the mercy of the elements, at the mercy of the wild animals, and had lost his authority over Satan and his demons.

On occasions, throughout history, there were men and women of God who appeared on the scene, realized that by obedience to God they could regain their spiritual authority, and exerted it. Joshua exerted it over the sun by commanding it to stand still. David exerted it over the wild animals by defeating them with his bare hands. But by and large man was helpless before Satan — until Jesus appeared on the scene.

Paul described Adam as a "pattern of one to come" (Romans 5:14). He called Jesus the "last Adam" and described Him as a "life-giving spirit." Thus in Jesus all dominion and spiritual authority was restored to mankind. In Christ man now has dominion, not only over this world, but over the spiritual world. Satan and all his demons are in submission to anyone who comes in the name of Jesus and in the power of His Holy Spirit.

The Authority of Jesus

Although Jesus was born the Son of God, full dominion was not His until He was baptized in the Holy Spirit at the time of His water baptism in the Jordan River. At that time Luke says Jesus was "full of the Holy Spirit" (Luke 4:1). Leaving the Jordan River, He went into His own wilderness exile — a time of fasting and praying for 40 days in the Judean wilderness. When He emerged, Luke says He "returned to Galilee in the *power* of the Spirit" (Luke 4:14). In other words, something happened to Jesus in the wilderness which empowered Him with spiritual authority.

Shortly after that, Jesus and His disciples boarded a small boat to cross the Sea of Galilee. After telling His disciples they were to go to the other side, He went to sleep in the stern. When a furious squall came up on the lake, threatening to capsize the boat, the disciples became frightened. They awoke Jesus who got up and took authority over the elements. He rebuked the wind and said to the waves, "Quiet! Be still!" Instantly the wind subsided and the water grew calm. Jesus then turned to His disciples and indicated they could have done the same things if they had faith — that is, if they had exerted authority in the name of Jesus (Mark 4:35-41).

Dominion Restored

This kind of thing happened a number of times. Jesus healed people and then told His disciples they could do the same thing. Gradually they began to catch on. One day they returned, after having been sent out by Jesus, and reported that they had taken authority and that not only had many people been healed, but they had been able to take dominion over the demons as well (Mark 6:7-13).

Following the resurrection of Jesus and His departure to heaven, the disciples were baptized in the same Spirit who raised Christ from the dead. At that time they suddenly realized that the same Spirit which raised Christ was dwelling in them — and that the authority of Jesus was now permanently theirs. They immediately began "doing the works" of Jesus, using His power and authority. In fact, all the miracles that Jesus performed, the disciples performed also.

That same authority, according to Jesus, is now ours. "These signs will accompany those who believe: In my name they will drive out demons; they will speak in new tongues, they will pick up snakes with their hands; and when they drink deadly poison, it will not hurt them at all; they will place their hands on sick people, and they will get well" (Mark 16:17-18). In other words, all believers should have authority over the elements, over the creatures of this earth, and over sickness. The authority God gave Adam has been returned to us through Jesus Christ.

The Authority of Moses

Paul says "death reigned from the time of Adam to the time of Moses." However, in the time of Moses, God reappeared and revealed Himself to His people through the Law given on Mt. Sinai. Moses, who was not only called "the Lawgiver" but was also obedient to God's Law, was one of those who — as a "type" of Christ — had dominion.

We see that authority contrasted with man's authority throughout the life of Moses. In his own life, he took human authority and tried to free the Hebrew slaves by killing a taskmaster. He failed at that and was banished into the wilderness of the Sinai. But when he returned to Egypt — 40 years later — he returned not in his own power but under the authority of God. Instead of using his wooden staff as a weapon (perhaps the same staff he had used to bash in the head of the Egyptian taskmaster), he used it as a symbol of God's power. In fact, from that time on, the staff of Moses was referred to as the "rod of God." He used it to show his authority before the Egyptian magicians, to hold out over the Nile River when it turned into blood, to hold over the Red Sea as the waters parted, to strike the rock and bring forth water, to hold over his head as the Israelites battled the Amalakites. Each time Moses took spiritual authority, showing his enemies and his friends what one righteous man was capable of doing in the name and in the power of God.

Lessons from the Wilderness

As a younger man, Moses thought he could correct all the injustice of Egypt — and the injustice of the desert — by using his staff as a weapon. But when God spoke to him and commissioned him to return to Egypt, He gave him a new authority. Moses was able to receive that authority because he had been humbled by the desert. Earlier he felt self-sufficient. When God spoke to him in the desert he had lost all self-sufficiency, going so far as to tell God he was unable to fulfill God's commission. God, however, had been forging a leader who did not need a club to take authority over Satan and his servants.

Here's an important lesson to remember: Spiritual leaders are never elected; they are called by God. When God calls, He also equips, and makes the ministry fruitful. From that time on, the badge of authority may be only a simple staff, but in the hands of a righteous man it becomes the rod of God.

Dominion Makes Us Conspicuous

When Moses returned to Pharaoh's court, after all those years in the wilderness, he did not come back as a prince — but as a shepherd. All the other leaders in Egypt carried swords or spears. But God told Moses to approach Pharaoh carrying his staff. He was to be deliberately conspicuous, out-of-place, so God's glory could be evident.

This is one of the prices of leadership. Moses could no longer act like a follower. He had been designated as a leader. But he was, like Jesus, a servant leader. He led by speaking the word of God, not by might or power.

God Calls Each of Us to Take Dominion

Often we shrink from the call of God, fearing it will deprive us of pleasure, cause us to be ridiculed, force us from the comforts of home into a rigorous life of discipline. We often equate God's call to take authority with going to our doom. But God does not call us to doom — instead He calls us to glory. When we rise in the name of Jesus, God's son, and take authority over Satan, over demons, over the things of this world which would prevent us from being conformed to the image of God's son, all hell quakes before us. Indeed, we have the same authority as God when we speak in Jesus' name.

CONCLUSIONS

1. The same authority God gave Adam over this earth has been restored to all believers through Jesus Christ.

2. God expects us to rule and reign over this world, taking dominion over sin, evil, sickness, the elements, even death.

3. Satan is powerless when faced with a believer who takes authority in the name of Jesus.

4. Whom God calls He also equips.

BIBLE STUDY

1. **Adam and Jesus**

    God created Adam in His own image. When He did this, He had a particular purpose in mind for man — a purpose different from all His other creatures.

    What kind of power did God give Adam and Eve? (Genesis 1:26-28)

    _____

    _____

    _____

NOTES

NOTES

When Adam sinned, he lost this authority. However, it was to be restored to mankind in a different form many years later.

How did Paul describe Adam? (Romans 5:14)

_____

Paul points out that through Adam all men were made sinners.

What does he say will happen when men accept Jesus? (Romans 5:19)

_____

What term does Paul use to describe Jesus? (I Corinthians 15:45)

_____

2. **The Authority of Moses**

When God called Moses, He gave him certain signs so Moses would never doubt God's authority. One of these signs involved Moses' staff.

What happened when Moses threw his staff on the ground? (Exodus 4:1-3)

_____

_____

God then showed Moses he had authority.

What did God tell Moses to do to teach him authority and what happened when he did it? (Exodus 4:4-5)

_____

_____

3. **Jesus Has All Authority**

In the Great Commission to His followers, Jesus told them something about Himself which they needed to know.

What did Jesus say He had which qualified Him to send them out? (Matthew 28:18)

_____

What happened at the water baptism of Jesus which gave Him power and authority? (Mark 1:10-11)

_____

_____

_____

Something happened to Jesus in the wilderness following His baptism. Compare Luke 4:1 with Luke 4:14 and describe the difference.

What is the difference between Luke 4:1 and Luke 4:14?

_____

_____

_____

After Jesus calmed the storm, the disciples in the boat with Him were "terrified."

What question did the disciples ask of themselves about Jesus? (Mark 4:41)

_____

_____

4. **Dominion of the Disciples**

   After Jesus had called His disciples and taught them some basic things about the Kingdom of God, He told them it was not enough for them to merely follow Him around. He wanted them to get active in His ministry. That meant doing the same things He was doing.

   What did Jesus tell His disciples they would be able to do when He transferred His power and authority to them? (Luke 9:1-2)

   _____

   _____

   _____

   What kind of results did these disciples have when they went out in the name of Jesus? (Mark 6:12-13)

   _____

   _____

   _____

5. **Spiritual Dominion of Today's Christian**

   Jesus said the miracles, which are evidence of the spiritual authority of the believer, were to continue on until He comes again to set up His final kingdom on earth.

   What five specific miracles did Jesus mention? (Mark 16:17-18)

   (1) _____
   (2) _____
   (3) _____
   (4) _____
   (5) _____

   To whom did Jesus say these things would happen? (Mark 16:16)

   _____

   There is a difference between faith and presumption. Presumption, for instance, would be to pick up a snake and dare it to bite you. Faith means if a snake attacks you, attempting to harm you while you are on a mission for God, you can take spiritual authority and not be harmed. There is an example of this in the book of Acts.

   What happened to Paul on the island of Malta and what was the result of his faith? (Acts 28:3-6)

   _____

   _____

NOTES

NOTES

What did Jesus say we would do because He went to Heaven and sent the Holy Spirit to each of us? (John 14:12)

_____

_____

PERSONAL REVIEW QUESTIONS

1. T F God told Moses to pick up the snake (which had once been his staff) to teach him that he had authority.
2. T F When God created Adam and Eve, He gave them full dominion over all the animals and plants in the Garden of Eden.
3. T F All mankind suffered because of Adam's sin.
4. T F The dominion God gave Adam and Eve will never be fully restored until Jesus sets up His final Kingdom on earth following His return.
5. T F God did not let Moses use his old staff since it was tainted with blood. Instead He created for him a new staff.
6. T F Jesus criticized His disciples after He stilled the storm because they didn't turn back when the waves got high.
7. T F Jesus implied His disciples could have stilled the storm themselves if they had exerted their faith.
8. T F Jesus only had partial authority while He was here on earth.
9. T F Jesus' disciples, following Pentecost, exerted the same authority Jesus had exerted.
10. T F God intends for all of us today to have the same authority Jesus had when He was on earth.
11. T F One way to exhibit our faith is by picking up poisonous snakes.
12. T F Jesus said all we had to do was believe, and the same signs and wonders which accompanied His ministry would accompany ours.

MEMORY VERSE

John 14:12 (Memorize, then write it on these lines.)

_____

_____

_____

TRUE OR FALSE ANSWERS

1.T, 2.T, 3.T, 4.F, 5.F, 6.F, 7.T, 8.F, 9.T, 10.T, 11.F, 12.T

Lesson 8
The Call of God: The Burning Bush
Hearing and Understanding God's Call on Our Lives

VIDEO REFERENCE: Lesson 8

Sometimes it takes a long time for God to work out His purposes in us. Moses had been in the Sinai forty years before he was able to get quiet enough to hear the call of God. During those preceding years, of course, God was cleansing his life, preparing him for that day when he would be able to hear — and submit to God's purpose for his life.

It happened one day at the base of Mt. Sinai, where Moses was herding sheep and goats for his father-in-law, Jethro. Moses had long since put aside any hope of returning to Egypt. His past was dead and, for all he knew, his old family was dead also. His brother, Aaron; his sister, Miriam (who had protected him from death when he was born) . . . all had been left behind. Even the great burden of his heart, the burden to see his Hebrew people set free from the bondage of slavery, had been left behind. Then on a special day God spoke to him out of a burning bush. He called him by name, identified Himself as God, and commissioned Moses to serve Him.

God Still Calls Today

The Bible is full of stories like this. God called Samuel when he was still a child, speaking to him in the darkness of the Temple and calling him to Himself. He sent Samuel as His ambassador to call David. He called the young man Isaiah who responded, "Here am I, send me." He called Saul as he was on the way to Damascus to kill Christians. Even Jesus spoke of God's call on His life when He stood in the synagogue in Nazareth and said, "The Spirit of the Lord is now upon me."

NOTES

God still calls us — not to specific tasks, but to Himself. There are those who mistakenly say they are "called to the ministry" or "called to a vocation." But the call of God is but one call. We are called to be "in Christ." Once we respond to that call, the Holy Spirit takes our various gifts, our natural endowments, the things we are talented to do, and appoints us to various places in the Kingdom where these can best glorify God.

The journey to spiritual maturity will always include a call — and a response.

CONCLUSIONS

1. God knows us and calls us by name.

2. Men often miss the call of God because they are in a hurry or because they have their ears tuned to other voices.

3. We are not called to specific tasks; we are called into Christ.

4. Each of us is gifted in specific areas. God uses these gifts once we respond to His call to satisfy our deepest longings, to build His body, and glorify Himself.

BIBLE STUDY

1. Called Into Christ

It is important to know that we are not called to special tasks or assignments. We are called to be in Christ. Once we are in Christ, then the Holy Spirit assigns us to various places in the body of Christ, using our gifted areas which have been part of our personality since we were created by God. Remember, Moses was a leader in Egypt long before he responded to God's call. The call of God is to submit to God's leadership. Then, once we become followers of God, the Holy Spirit uses our "natural" abilities for God's glory, rather than for our own glory.

When Paul visited Rome he said God had authorized him to call people. To what were they called? (Romans 1:5)

These Romans had previously belonged to Caesar. To whom were they now called to belong? (Romans 1:6)

What is to be the title of these who are called? (Romans 1:7)

---

2. Called By His Name

Once we are "in Christ" the world recognizes us as different. It is as though we have been branded — as slave owners once branded their slaves to show ownership. Because He has called us by our name — that is, invited us to Himself — we now belong to Him.

Once we have been redeemed and God has called us, to whom do we belong? (Isaiah 43:1)

When He calls us by name, what does He give us? (Isaiah 45:4)

_____

By what name are the followers of God called? (Jeremiah 14:9; 15:16)

_____

3. **The Calling of God**

   The journey to spiritual maturity is described in the Bible as a **race**. We are not racing against each other but racing against ourselves and against the power of Satan, who is constantly trying to trip us up and hold us back. We have been called by God to win, however. We are not predestined to be losers, nor are we left to run the race in our own strength. Our task is to run the best we can in the strength of the Holy Spirit. Our high calling is that we shall indeed finish the race and be declared winners. (See Philippians 3:13-14)

   In the process of running the race toward spiritual maturity, we discover that we are called to live a particular kind of life.

   What kind of life are we called to live? (II Timothy 1:9)

   _____

   How is this calling described in Hebrews 3:1?

   _____

   Peter says that those who answer God's call are "elected" — or chosen — to be one with Him for all eternity. If we abide in Christ our calling and election is certain.

   What rewards are promised to those whose calling is sure? (II Peter 1:11-12)

   _____

   _____

   _____

4. **The Called**

   Jesus says "many are called, few are chosen" (Matthew 22:14). Corrie ten Boom once described this by saying the Kingdom of God is entered through a swinging door. As we approach the door it says, "Called." If we enter the door — that is, if we respond to God's invitation — and glance back, we'll see on the other side of that door the classification "Chosen." Those who answer God's call are numbered among God's chosen.

   God has a purpose for those who answer His call. If we love God what does He do with all the circumstances of life? (Romans 8:28)

   _____

   _____

5. **All Are Called**

   God does not limit His call to any one group or culture. Instead, all are called to exhibit the power of Christ and the wisdom of God. In I Corinthians 1:24 Paul talks of two nationalities in particular — which included all the people in that particular area — whom God had called.

NOTES

NOTES

Who are the two nationalities Paul told the Corinthians God had called to be followers of Christ? (I Corinthians 1:22-25)

_____

The Corinthian Christians were concerned about their self-worth. Paul writes to them to encourage them, to remind them that God has indeed called them to a special task — that of revealing Jesus Christ to their friends and associates. He points out that God loves to call "common" people to uncommon tasks; He calls natural people to do the supernatural.

What kind of people were the Corinthians before God called them? (I Corinthians 1:26-28)

_____

_____

_____

_____

What kind of life were these Corinthians called to live? (I Corinthians 1:2)

_____

When God called the Corinthians, He called them into a relationship. What kind of relationship was this? (I Corinthians 1:9)

_____

_____

6. Called To Be Free

The call of God is a call to submit ourselves to Jesus Christ. This call separates us from the call of the world, which had a former claim on our lives. In writing to the Corinthians, Paul reminds them that some of them were once homosexuals, adulterers, thieves and murderers. That was the call of the world, and they were unable to break that call in their own strength. But when they answered God's call, they received power to turn their backs on the ways of the world and walk in a new way.

The same was true of those Jews who had once been in bondage to the old Law. They felt obligated to try to keep the Law, even if it made them miserable and killed them. But when they answered God's call, they received power — not to break the Law, but to live by the spirit of the Law rather than the bondage of the letter of the Law.

Christians then are called to _____ **and to use that freedom to** _____.

(Galatians 5:13)

7. The Universal Calling of God

Paul described himself as a prisoner of the Lord, yet he said he was called to be free. His "slavery" to Christ had set him free from being a slave to sin and of being a slave to the Law and tradition. His freedom is evidenced by the fact he is now free to be himself — the way God made him. Once we are "liberated" from the bondage of this world, we can begin to exercise our natural gifts and talents without shame and intimidation. This will be evidenced by the fruit of the Holy Spirit in our lives.

List these fruit of the Spirit. (Galatians 5:22-23)

(1) _____
(2) _____
(3) _____
(4) _____
(5) _____
(6) _____
(7) _____
(8) _____
(9) _____

When the Holy Spirit is active in our lives — and He should be active from the time we respond to God's call to become a Christian — we come into unity with all others who have responded to God's call. Paul talks of this unity in Ephesians 4, saying you were "called to one hope when you were called." He then describes that hope as the hope of unity — "one Lord, one faith, one baptism, one God and Father of all." In short, we are not called to be diverse or to function differently. We are called into the one body of Christ.

Once in the body of Christ, however, the Holy Spirit then activates our gifts — those things which we are naturally endowed to do. When this is done, we begin to feel a deep inner satisfaction, a sense of fulfillment.

What will God give us when we delight ourselves in the Lord? (Psalm 37:4)

_____

These natural gifts, or endowments (you may wish to call them a deeper inner longing or the desire of your heart), are meant to be used in the body of Christ. Although each of us is called to one body, we are to function differently once we are in that body — just as the arm functions differently from the leg. We see this evidenced in the various "offices" of the body of Christ. Paul says we are not supposed to fill all the offices, just the one to which we are especially suited — the one in which we are gifted.

What are the offices Paul mentions in Ephesians 4:11?

(1) _____
(2) _____
(3) _____
(4) _____ and _____

We see this same principle again in I Corinthians 12. Here Paul tells the Corinthians that although they are all called to a universal calling — to be "in Christ" — each individual Christian will function differently.

Paul says each of us will have what kind of gifts? (I Corinthians 12:4)

_____

Using these different gifts God appoints us to different functions in the church.

NOTES

What are the gifted functions listed by Paul in I Corinthians 12:27-28?

(1) _____

(2) _____

(3) _____

(4) _____

(5) _____

(6) _____

(7) _____

(8) _____

What are the two things Paul says are irrevocable? (Romans 11:29)

(1) _____

(2) _____

8. **Results of Being Called**

    We are called into Christ. That means we let Jesus Christ take over the rule of our lives. He not only rules our lives, but we then become partakers of His life as well. Sometimes this is not so pleasant, for it means we will walk the same kind of life He walked.

    What could be the result of this calling while we are here on earth? (I Peter 2:20-21)

    _____

    Since our calling is out of the world, which brings only death, and into Christ who is called the "lifegiver," we can now lay claim to a precious final result.

    What was given to us — what we are called to — when we made our confession that Jesus Christ is Lord? (I Timothy 6:12)

    _____

    This same promise is repeated in the book of Hebrews.

    What are those who are called destined to receive? (Hebrews 9:15)

    _____

    The word "called" also means "invited." When God called us He invited us to be partakers not only of His suffering, but of His resurrection glory.

    To what are "the called" invited? (Revelation 19:9)

    _____

PERSONAL REVIEW QUESTIONS

1. T   F   When God spoke to Moses out of the burning bush, He not only called Moses by name, He also identified Himself.

2. T   F   God told Moses to take his shoes off because the ground was holy.

3. T   F   God's call to Moses was the last time God called anyone by name.

4. T   F   God only calls Jews to follow Him.

5. T   F   We are not called to special ministries; we are called to be in Christ.

6. T F Only 144,000 will be called to inherit eternal life.

7. T F Once God gives us gifts, He will never take them away because they are irrevocable.

8. T F The call of the world results in death, but the call of God results in life.

9. T F Once we answer God's call, our days of suffering are over.

10. T F God has a purpose for each of us.

11. T F We should all seek the highest offices in the church since this will indicate to God we have high standards.

12. T F Since we are called to freedom, we no longer have to be under the bondage of being a slave to Christ.

MEMORY VERSE

Romans 8:28 (Memorize, then write it on these lines)

_____

_____

_____

_____

NOTES

TRUE OR FALSE ANSWERS

1-T, 2-T, 3-F, 4-F, 5-T, 6-T, 7-T, 8-T, 9-F, 10-T, 11-F, 12-F

Lesson 9
Hospitality: Learning to Give
God's People are Generous People

VIDEO REFERENCE: Lesson 9

One of the great needs of mankind is the need to belong to a family. When Moses was forced to flee from Egypt into the wilderness, he left behind his family. For forty years his family had been the Egyptian royalty. As an infant he had been adopted by the Pharaoh's daughter — although for the first several years of his life he was nursed and cared for by his own mother. But all this was left behind when he was forced into his wilderness exile.

Filled with despair and confusion, the once-prince of Egypt staggered into the burning crucible of the wilderness until he came to an oasis. There he slept until awakened by human voices. It was his first personal encounter with the people of the desert — very similar to the Bedouin who still live in today's Sinai. That evening he spent the night in the tent of an old Bedouin sheik, or chieftain — a man called Jethro. Later Moses would marry Jethro's daughter, Zipporah, who would bear him two sons. However, equally important to his relationship with Zipporah was his relationship with old Jethro, for from him he would learn how to survive in the desert — an ability which would make it possible for him later to lead the Israelites from Egypt to the borders of Canaan.

How To Survive In The Wilderness

The secret of desert survival is generosity. There are no strangers in the wilderness — just friends you haven't met. Everyone shares. You have to if you are going to live. Jethro surprised Moses that first night by inviting him into his tent for a meal — and by providing a place for him to sleep. "Where is he?" Jethro asked his daughters who had only met Moses at the oasis. "Why did you leave him? Invite him to have something to eat" (Exodus 2:20). In this simple act of generosity and sharing, Moses began to learn something, not only of desert survival but of the ways of God — for God is a god of wilderness places.

It was Jethro who taught Moses about the god El — who was totally unlike the gods of the Egyptians Moses was familiar with. "El is at the center of all being," Jethro told Moses. "He is the God of our father Abraham, and the God of your ancestor Jacob. He is known to us as *El Elohe* — the Most High God."

It was God, Moses discovered, who made men like Jethro generous. Men of God are always generous. Stinginess is the way of death. Generosity — especially among those who are wandering in the wilderness — is the way of life.

Code of the Desert

This unwritten code of hospitality — generosity — is still practiced in the Sinai. It originated with Abraham who was called "the father of hospitality." It was Abraham who first decreed that the essentials of life were never to be denied any wilderness pilgrim, be he friend or enemy. The Bedouin of today's Sinai still welcome weary pilgrims — total strangers — into their tents with the greeting, *"Ahlan Wa Sahlan"* — "You are part of the family."

This code of hospitality recognizes that no man can exist alone in the wilderness. It is one of the deep truths learned in tough times. We are not only forced to lean on each other for help, but we are obligated to reach out to the stranger who knocks at our door — even though we are as poor as he.

The wells of the desert, even though they have been dug by the hard labor of one man, belong to anyone who is thirsty. No one ever puts a wall around a well. The same is true of shade. A person can die in the desert sun, so shade — whether it be your tree or your tent — is free to anyone who has a need. Also, on a cold night or in the winter the warmth of a fire belongs to anyone who is cold. And a warm cup of tea or broth is always offered — even though you may have to divide your last serving with a stranger. The reason? Every desert dweller knows that "there, but for the grace of God, go I." Next time it could be he who is thirsty, dying of heat, or in need of food and shelter. So, long before Jesus said it in the Sermon on the Mount, the desert dweller — having listened to God in the desperation of the wilderness — learned to put into practice the Golden Rule. For the sake of survival one must do unto others what he would have done unto him.

God's Law Commands Generosity

What Moses learned first from old Jethro and then by living in the wilderness 40 years, God knew should be taught to the Israelites. Even though those Children of Israel were not to dwell forever in the Sinai, nevertheless God knew that because they were to be a people set apart, different, holy, they would always be persecuted. Persecution means they would always be, to some degree, wilderness people. They would be forced from their homes and homeland. They would have to live in catacombs, in ghettos, as wanderers and pilgrims. They needed to learn how to be hospitable, how to be generous. For if a man is stingy, if he hoards for himself what others need, then one day he himself shall be without.

Therefore when God spoke the Law into existence, He told Moses to major on generosity and hospitality. Nowhere is this more evident than in God's command concerning the tithe. God told the Israelites to give away ten percent of everything they earned. Since money was not a medium of exchange, the Israelites were to tithe the "first fruits" of their harvest. This included the calves and lambs as well as the grain offerings. These tithes were brought to a central storehouse where the priests — elders in the tribe of Levi — would distribute them to the needy.

The Tithe

Actually, tithing was not a new practice. Abraham had given tithes to Melchizedek, king of Salem. Jacob had promised God a tithe of all his income. All Moses did was make certain every Israelite recognized the validity of this way of life. In Leviticus 27:30-32, we find that all the tithe of the land, whether of the seed of the land or of the fruit of the tree, is the Lord's; it is holy unto the Lord.

There were three sorts of tithes required of the people.

(1) To the Levites for their maintenance (Numbers 18:21, 24).

(2) For the Lord's feasts and sacrifices, to be eaten in a place which the Lord should choose to put His name there. Later this tithe was sent to Jerusalem (Deuteronomy 14:22-24).

(3) Besides these two, there was to be, every third year, a tithe for the poor — to be eaten in their own dwellings (Deuteronomy 14:28-29).

The Levites, after receiving tithes from the people, were commanded to return ten per cent of this to the Lord by giving it to Aaron, the high priest (Numbers 18:26, 28).

Jesus and Giving

Later Jesus commended those religious Jews who tithed (Matthew 23:23) but was angry because they had made tithing a law — a religious rite — rather than understanding the spirit behind the original Law, which was to guarantee that we, as God's people, would be generous. In fact, on several occasions Jesus pointed out that many of the religious Jews tithed their income but oppressed the poor, the widows, and the orphans. It did no good to tithe as far as God was concerned (assuming the Jews were tithing to gain God's favor) if they did not practice the "weightier matters" of the law concerning justice and righteousness.

Jesus said we should certainly tithe — for it is a constant reminder of God's requirement for generosity — but we should not leave the other undone, for that was the primary reason for the tithe — to remind us to be generous and hospitable with *all* our belongings.

However, there is an even deeper reason God wants His people to be hospitable and generous. God, by His very nature, is a giver. God's basic characteristic is love. Love always gives — without expecting or wanting anything in return. Love gives because love is generous. In fact, in the old translation of the Bible love is often translated as "charity" — the word we use for giving without wanting anything in return. God gives good gifts. He gave us His son, Jesus, as a perfect sacrifice for our sins. He gives, and gives, and gives again. There is no limit to His mercy, His compassion, His loving-kindness, His forgiveness. God wants us to be like Him. When we give, we take on a part of His nature.

CONCLUSIONS

1. Hospitality and generosity are necessary if we are to survive — for we are all part of one family.

2. Tithing was commanded to remind us to be generous.

3. Tithing should not become an end to itself. God's highest command is that we live generous and hospitable lives.

4. God is a god of love. The primary characteristic of love is giving, or generosity. God wants His followers to give so we may be like Him.

BIBLE STUDY

1. The Nature of God

Everyone who has ever established a relationship with God has taken on the nature of hospitality and generosity. It is impossible for a man to love God and not love his fellow man.

What did Jesus say was the greatest kind of love? (John 15:13)

_____

_____

Jesus also pointed out there were two great commandments. All of God's Law and all of the teachings of the Old Testament prophets centered around these two commandments. Jesus pointed out they are alike; in fact, it is impossible to separate them.

What are the two great commandments? (Matthew 22:37-39)

(1) _____

_____

(2) _____

_____

Jesus' follower, and perhaps His closest friend while he was on earth, later wrote a letter to the young church in which he urged them to love one another. "For love is of God," he said.

Where did the apostle John say love comes from? (I John 4:7)

_____

Is it possible to love God without showing that love to our fellow human beings through giving? (I John 2:9-11)

_____

Faith in God is not really faith unless it is accompanied by generosity toward those in need. James writes that it is not enough to say to a cold, hungry person, "God bless you." Since we are to have the nature of God, then we should expect God to bless that person THROUGH US. We are to minister to a person's physical needs as well as his spiritual needs.

How does James describe faith without works? (James 2:17)

_____

How did God show His love to this world? (I John 4:9)

_____

_____

_____

Since God loves us, what does He expect us to do? (I John 4:11)

_____

2. Desert Hospitality

God had a purpose for sending Moses into the desert. That purpose was to

NOTES

learn about God. The first person, therefore, that God sent into Moses' life became one of his most influential friends. From him Moses would learn the ways of the desert but, more important, would begin to understand something of the nature of God. The Bible calls this same man by two names: Reuel and Jethro. Probably his real name was Jethro — which means "preeminence" — for he was a tribal leader or chieftain. On the other hand, when Moses recalled the story of their first meeting and wrote it down in what is now the book of Exodus, he gave him another name as well: Reuel. That name means "friend of God."

What did Reuel (Jethro) do which exhibited the nature of God? (Exodus 2:20)

_____

_____

Later, as Reuel extended his giving nature, he presented Moses with an even more precious gift. What was that gift? (Exodus 2:21)

_____

_____

3. Giving as Part of the Law

At Mt. Sinai, 40 years following Moses' first encounter with Jethro, God began to teach all the people about giving. Since they knew nothing of this concept, He wrote it in the Law — commanding that which He would later write on their hearts through Jesus Christ.

How much did God command the people to give and what was it called? (Leviticus 27:30-32)

_____

_____

Under the Law every child of God was commanded to give three tithes.

List the three tithes.

(1) (Numbers 18:21, 24) _____

_____

(2) (Deuteronomy 14:22-24) _____

_____

(3) (Deuteronomy 14:28-29) _____

_____

The Levites, who received one of the tithes from the people, were commanded to give ten percent of all they received back to the Lord. To whom did this go? (Numbers 18:28)

_____

4. Jesus and Giving

Jesus not only had much to say about giving, He was a gift Himself — the product of God's nature. Remember: "God so loved the world that He *gave* His only begotten son..." (John 3:16).

What did Jesus say about tithing? (Matthew 23:23)

_____

_____

_____

5. God Our Source and Supply

Tithing forces us to rely upon God. It does not make earthly sense to give away hard-earned money and supplies. However, as we go against human nature by forcing ourselves to tithe, we gradually begin to write God's law on our heart. In fact, we become like God who is the great giver. We are also forced to realize that God is our source — not man. When we start living God's way — the way of generosity, hospitality and giving — then God blesses us. In short, when we give, we receive.

What does God say He will do when His people obey Him and tithe their income? (Malachi 3:10)

_____

_____

_____

If we give what will happen to us in return? (Luke 6:38)

_____

_____

Although it may seem that we deplete our money supply when we give, God says He will miraculously resupply that reservoir from His own storehouse. The life of giving, of being hospitable, of sharing — which begins with our tithing — puts us in the proper position to receive God's blessing.

Who can we expect to supply all our needs? (Philippians 4:19)

_____

PERSONAL REVIEW QUESTIONS

1. T F   Reuel was Jethro's father-in-law.
2. T F   God commanded the Israelites to tithe because the church needed money.
3. T F   The priests who received the tithe could do with it whatever they wanted.
4. T F   Jesus told the Jews they didn't have to tithe anymore.
5. T F   God wanted His followers to be generous because He is generous.
6. T F   Love always gives.
7. T F   Although we are to give without wanting anything in return, God does promise that those who give will be blessed.
8. T F   When we give, we put ourselves in a position to receive God's blessings.
9. T F   Jesus excused the religious Jews for their oppression of others because they were good tithers.

NOTES

10. T   F   All God wants from us is to tell those in need that God loves them.
11. T   F   All those who are like God will be generous.
12. T   F   It is impossible to love God and not love our fellow man.

MEMORY VERSE

Luke 6:38 (Memorize, then write it on these lines)

_____

_____

_____

_____

TRUE OR FALSE ANSWERS

1-F, 2-F, 3-F, 4-F, 5-T, 6-T, 7-T, 8-T, 9-F, 10-F, 11-T, 12-T

Lesson 10
The Law: Lessons from Mt. Sinai
Learning the Nature of God

VIDEO REFERENCE: Lesson 10

God's intent for the Israelites was that they should no longer be slaves but should become a nation. A nation is a group of people under government. Governments run by laws. The purpose of this chosen nation was to introduce the Messiah to all nations. The Messiah, in turn, would reveal God. Thus, the reason God brought the Israelites to Mt. Sinai and gave them the Law was to reveal His nature.

The Torah

The Hebrew word for law is *torah*. It is a commandment from a person of higher authority to a lower one. Torah could be the law of a father over his household, the education given by a mother to her children, the direction of a priest concerning spiritual matters, the command of a military officer, the dictate of a king, or, in its highest form, the Law of God for His people. When the Children of Israel gathered at the base of Mt. Sinai, it was a sacred and holy moment. Until that time God had only spoken to individuals. Now He was getting ready to speak to an entire nation — and bring them under the Law. Before they received the Law, they had to cleanse themselves. There were various rites which God put them through. They were not even allowed to touch the base of Mt. Sinai, for it was considered holy. When the Law was given, it was accompanied by terrifying dramatics: earthquake, lightning, volcanic eruptions and sudden darkness. It was God's way of saying to the people: I am giving you my most precious and sacred gift. I am revealing myself.

It seems strange that God would reveal Himself in commandments when He knew the people could not keep them. Aaron, the high priest, broke the second commandment even before the tablets of stone were given to the people. Moses broke the third commandment at Kadesh Barnea when he disobediently struck the rock to bring forth water and did it in the name of the Lord. Every one of the ten commandments was broken by the Israelites the day they received them. The people simply did not have the necessary power to live by the Law.

Of course, God did not give the commandments expecting the people to be able to keep them. Rather, He gave them to reveal His nature. For God is far more interested in a people who want to establish a relationship with Him than in a people who keep all the rules but never learn to abide in His presence.

Rules for Living a Happy, Healthy Life

The Law covered every aspect of life. There was the criminal law covering things like murder, assault, theft, kidnapping, negligence and damage. Then there were laws dealing with the moral and religious side of life. Other laws concerned the family. There were even laws which dealt with the behavior and the treatment of slaves. Some laws covered diet, others sexual relations, sanitation, government, money, agriculture and, most important, worship. God was taking a group of people who had known nothing but slavery for 400 years, and was molding them into a nation.

More important, God was revealing Himself to the Israelites through His Law. The Israelites were finally free from Egyptian slavery, but they were not free to do anything they wanted. They were free to do what God wanted. And until they wanted to do what God wanted, they would remain under the Law. Granted, the Law was highly restrictive — it was filled with "thou shalt nots" — but these restrictions were designed to help the people channel their creativity toward God, rather than to destroy their creativity and individuality. Very patiently, very gently — and sometimes with sternness — God brought these people to Himself. He showed them that in order to have complete freedom they had to be a people under absolute authority, for true happiness comes only when we are in submission to the will of God. And to these people the only way they knew the will of God was through the Law.

Purpose of the Law

The laws were given to extol the mercy of the Lord. The laws were binding in that if broken the Covenant between God and man was broken. The result was a broken relationship between God and man, leaving man floundering alone in darkness and death — cut off from light and life. It was — and is — ample motive to try to keep the Law.

The keeping of the Law was — and is — necessary to secure the blessing of the Lord. These laws have a twofold character: they promote love to God and love to one's neighbor.

Jesus and the Law

Twelve hundred years later the Messiah arrived on the scene. As with the giving of the Law, His arrival was accompanied by phenomena in nature. He came, not to do away with the Law, but to fulfill it. In fact, Jesus was called "the Lawgiver" because of His respect for the Mosaic Law.

By the time Jesus arrived on earth, however, the religious leaders of the Jews had twisted the Law to give it a meaning quite different from God's original meaning. In their effort to please God, they had written huge commentaries on the Law. These commentaries, called *Talmud*, reflected man's understanding of the Law — and man's means of enforcing it. The Law, instead of being the means by which God was revealed, revealed only man's nature. Instead of the Law being a servant to man, as God had originally intended, man had become a slave to the law. It was not the Law which was wrong, it was man's method of keeping it. Man insisted on keeping the letter while Jesus said God, who looked on the heart, was more interested in the spirit of the Law.

Paul said the Law is the reflection of God's own perfection. It is the transcript of God's holiness. The Law shows us God's desire for our thought and behavior. Peter said we were to be holy in all manner of life because God had called us to be holy. Salvation, then, means being saved from breaking the Law. That means we are saved to be holy — to keep the Law.

The major difference between the pilgrims in the Old Testament and the saints in the New Testament is the presence of Jesus Christ and the power of the Holy Spirit. Jesus reveals God totally. He adds love to the Law. The Holy Spirit gives us the desire to keep the Law. Even though we are still incapable of keeping it in our own strength, the indwelling presence of the Holy Spirit gives us a new desire. He transforms our minds and gives us the desire to be like Jesus, who walked in both the perfect letter and the perfect spirit of the Law of God.

CONCLUSIONS

1. God gave the Law from Mt. Sinai to reveal Himself.

2. God's Law is still in effect, although it must be interpreted in the light of the teachings and the spirit of Jesus who totally fulfilled the Law.

3. Man was and is incapable of obeying the letter of the Law. However, the Holy Spirit gives us the desire to obey.

4. God looks upon the heart rather than on our behavior record.

BIBLE STUDY

1. The Ten Commandments

The Ten Commandments, which contained the original Law, are the heart and center of all God's laws given in the Old Testament. They were given by God to Moses who in turn delivered them to the nation of Israel.

List the Ten Commandments as found in Exodus 20.

1. (Exodus 20:3) _____

2. (Exodus 20:4) _____

3. (Exodus 20:7) _____

_____

4. (Exodus 20:8) _____

_____

5. (Exodus 20:12) _____

6. (Exodus 20:13) _____

7. (Exodus 20:14) _____

8. (Exodus 20:15) _____

NOTES

9. (Exodus 20:16) _____

10. (Exodus 20:17) _____

Which is the only commandment that contains a specific promise of punishment? What is that punishment? (Exodus 20:4-5)

_____

_____

_____

Which is the only commandment that contains a promise of reward? What is that reward? (Exodus 20:12)

_____

_____

2. **Summary of the Law**

   What, according to Jesus, is the two-fold purpose of the Law? (Matthew 22:37-40)

   (1) _____

   (2) _____

3. **Jesus and the Law**

   Jesus kept the Law of Moses. He told His followers they should keep it also. He said He had not come to abolish the Law — but to fulfill it. He said the Law was here forever, for it reflected the nature of God. He warned against any kind of teaching which nullified the Law or encouraged people to break it.

   How did Jesus describe those who broke the Law and taught others to break it? (Matthew 5:19)

   _____

   Paul lists several of the commandments and says they can all be summed up in one rule.

   What rule sums up these specific commandments? (Romans 13:9)

   _____

   What is the fulfillment of the Law? (Romans 13:10)

   _____

   Keeping the commandments is stressed throughout the Bible — especially in the New Testament.

   What does the Apostle John say obeying the commandments signifies? (I John 2:3)

   _____

What is a man called who says he loves God but deliberately breaks the commandments? (I John 2:4)

___

Jesus reinforced the necessity of keeping the commandments by referring to His own example of keeping the Father's commandments and thus abiding in the Father's love.

What specific command did Jesus say He had received from His Father which He intended to keep? (John 10:17-18)

___

___

What will happen to us if we obey God's commands the way Jesus obeyed God's commands? (John 15:10)

___

___

Paul confessed that he was unable to keep the Law. Although he wanted to keep it, he said, he kept doing evil. He described it as a great battle constantly raging in his inner being. However, he rejoiced in one particular thing.

What did Paul say was his utmost delight? (Romans 7:22)

___

Jesus warned against allowing the Law to become our god. We serve only one god, he said, and should not allow God's Law to become a substitute god. The Law was given to help us serve God, not to become the god of our service.

He specifically pointed out the law concerning the Sabbath. According to the fourth commandment, the seventh day was to be a day of rest, in which no secular work was to be done, and which was to be kept holy to God. At a later time the Jewish elders added rules and regulations until the Sabbath rules became burdensome, and, in some cases, foolish. It was against this, and not against God's law of the Sabbath, that Jesus set Himself in His teaching and healing.

For whom did Jesus say the Sabbath was made to help and bless? (Mark 2:27)

___

In the Sermon on the Mount, Jesus referred to a number of the laws. One law, in particular, caught the people's attention. He talked about the seventh commandment — "Thou shalt not commit adultery" — and pointed out that merely refraining from the physical act of adultery did not mean a person had kept the commandment.

How did Jesus describe adultery to the men? (Matthew 5:27-28)

___

___

The Apostle Paul was deeply concerned that the Christians in the region of Galatia were trying to enforce the Jewish laws. He reminded them they had begun in the spirit, but were now going back to the letter of the Law.

NOTES

NOTES

What did Paul call these Galatians? (Galatians 3:1,3)

_____

He goes on to say that we are not justified before God because we obey the Law (for no man can fully obey the Law). Now our faith must be in Christ, not in the Law — although we are to continue to desire to obey all the Law.

From what did Christ redeem us? (Galatians 3:13)

_____

PERSONAL REVIEW QUESTIONS

1. T F Although the Ten Commandments were given to be obeyed, the other laws God gave from Mt. Sinai were relative.

2. T F After God gave the Law from Mt. Sinai, He never revealed Himself again.

3. T F Since the Israelites could not keep the commandments, God sent Jesus to tell us all we had to do was love one another and not worry about the Law.

4. T F Jesus said there was only one command that we needed to pay attention to: to love God with all our hearts.

5. T F Paul called the Galatians foolish because they were teaching people to love the Law and to try to obey it.

6. T F Paul called the Galatians foolish because they believed they could please God without keeping the Law.

7. T F Paul called the Galatians foolish because they were trying to put people back under the Law rather than leading them to faith in Christ.

8. T F Jesus said we should want to keep all the Law.

9. T F Jesus condemned those who taught people to forsake the Law.

10. T F God gave the Law from Mt. Sinai to reveal His nature.

11. T F Jesus said the Sabbath had become a great burden on the people and they no longer had to feel they should go to church on Sunday.

12. T F Since wanting to commit adultery is just as bad as the act, we might as well go ahead and commit the act.

MEMORY VERSE

Matthew 22:37-39 (Memorize, then write it on these lines.)

_____

_____

_____

_____

TRUE OR FALSE ANSWERS

1.F, 2.F, 3.F, 4.F, 5.F, 6.F, 7.T, 8.T, 9.T, 10.T, 11.F, 12.F

Lesson 11
Pilgrims: Staying Under the Cloud
Trusting God Day by Day

VIDEO REFERENCE: Lesson 11

Although God had appointed Moses as leader of the Israelites, He had also said His ultimate intention was for them to be a nation of priests. A priest is a man who hears from God. God appreciates organization. But His highest intention for His children is not that they just hear the voice of a leader and follow him, but that all of them also learn to hear the voice of God. Each believer is to learn to function as a "follower" of God as well.

From the moment the Israelites left Egypt until they finally entered the Promised Land, God accompanied them in a cloud during the day — and a pillar of fire at night. *"In all the travels of the Israelites, whenever the cloud lifted from above the Tabernacle, they would set out; but if the cloud did not lift, they did not set out — until the day it lifted"* (Exodus 40:36-37). These natural phenomena were evidences of the presence of God. But more than being a reminder of God's presence, they were guides. God was teaching His people how to trust Him for their daily walk. It is the lesson every pilgrim on his way to spiritual maturity must learn.

In the desert we find three kinds of people:

Hermits are those who move in from the outside, settle in caves, and stay in one place until they die.

Nomads are people on the move — like today's Bedouin — but they never go anywhere. They move in circles, always winding up where they began.

Pilgrims are not desert dwellers. They do not belong in the desert. They are simply passing through from one place to another.

God's people are designed to be pilgrims. And all of life, to some degree, is a wilderness experience. But the trek through the wilderness is a passage through trouble, not a place to stop and wallow in adversity. Deserts are not designed to choke the life from us; rather they are designed by God to mold us and shape us into the image of His Son. Remember the old Negro spiritual: "This world is not my home, I'm just a-passing through."

Staying On The Move

To keep His people moving, to keep them from becoming stagnant, God kept the cloud in motion. It was placed over the Tabernacle itself — the tent of meeting that contained the Ark of the Covenant. As long as the cloud was stationary, the people remained in that place. When the cloud moved, they folded their tents, dismantled the Tabernacle, packed all their belongings and moved out under the cloud. Sometimes the cloud remained stationary for long periods. At other times it may have moved daily. But *"at the Lord's command they encamped, and at the Lord's command they set out"* (Numbers 9:23). They were learning, in the words of an old hymn, to "trust and obey."

Hermits become self-conscious rather than God-conscious and other-conscious. As we move to spiritual maturity we pass through wildernesses which force us to get our eyes off ourselves and onto God and others. If we are going to make it in life we'll have to do it as a group — and with our eyes focused on God.

The only time a wilderness experience becomes a tragedy is when we fail to understand that the purpose of adversity is to force us to look to God. When we understand that God has enrolled us in the "School of the Wilderness" for a season only — for specific reasons — we can even enjoy the passage. It is then we realize we do not pass through the desert alone. Psalm 23 is the pilgrim's song, for it teaches us there are tables in the wilderness, there is oil for healing, there is protection, and that God goes with us — even through the valley of the shadow of death.

The Need For A Guide

To be lost in the desert without a guide means almost certain death. The guide not only shows us the way but knows where we can find food, water and shade. Every wilderness wanderer needs a guide — someone who has been this way before.

Moses was such a guide for the Israelites. For 40 years he had lived in the Sinai. He knew every wadi, every spring, every place of safety. Without him the Exodus would never have taken place. Moses, however, was limited. Moses knew that after the group reached Mt. Sinai and started north toward Kadesh Barnea, he would soon run out of familiar territory. Therefore, he persuaded his brother-in-law, Hobab, who was an expert guide and tracker, to go with them into the Promised Land. Hobab was the son of Jethro, and brother to Moses' wife, Zipporah. Hobab consented and became the "eyes" of Moses. Although Moses still looked to the cloud for overall guidance, he looked to Hobab for day-by-day help.

While each of us should be dependent upon God's guidance in our trek through the wilderness toward spiritual maturity, there is also the need for human assistance — spiritual directors, so to speak. The idea is to follow our earthly leaders but at the same time keep our eye on the cloud.

CONCLUSIONS

1. God is more interested in whether we obey Him on the journey than whether we reach our goal.
2. God wants us to stay on the move, always open to change, constantly growing into the likeness of His Son, Jesus Christ.

3. Although we are to be individual priests, each answerable to God, we also need spiritual leaders to guide us toward spiritual maturity.

BIBLE STUDY

1. Following the Cloud

The Israelites were a people on the move. God did not want them to get comfortable in the wilderness, build permanent structures, and settle down. For many generations they had been "settled" in Egypt, taking orders from slave-masters. Now God wanted their roots firmly planted in Him. They were to become a nation of priests. That meant they had to learn to follow God on a daily basis.

What discipline did God use to teach the Israelites how to follow Him? (Exodus 40:36-37)

_____

_____

At whose command did the Israelites move? (Numbers 9:23)

_____

Each time the cloud moved Moses would have all the Israelites fold their tents and prepare to move. Then the Levites would pick up the Ark of the Covenant. At that time Moses would cry out a great battle cry.

What was the battle cry of Moses? (Numbers 10:35)

_____

_____

God's mercies are given to all those who obey Him. How frequently should we expect His mercies and what time of day will we first notice them? (Lamentations 3:23)

_____

_____

How are we to wait on God's direction? (Lamentations 3:26)

_____

2. Obstacles On the Path to Spiritual Maturity

The journey to spiritual maturity is not a smooth, easy one. We can understand why God's mercies are needed "fresh every morning," for we need them to help us through the tough times which seem to come daily.

What does Job say we should expect as surely as the sparks of a fire fly upward? (Job 5:7)

_____

However, despite the fact we face constant trouble, the mature Christian soon learns there is purpose to every obstacle he encounters along the way.

NOTES

NOTES

How are we to face these obstacles? What should be our attitude? (James 1:2)

_____

If our faith is tried (tested) what will we learn? (James 1:3)

_____

As we look at the Israelite pilgrims trudging their way through the wilderness, we see a reflection of our own lives in each obstacle they encounter — and we see the reflection of human nature's reaction to those obstacles.

How did the Israelites react when they ran out of water and were faced with the same diet of manna each day? (Numbers 21:5)

_____

What did God do to teach the Israelites a lesson in obedience? (Numbers 21:6)

_____

How did the people react when confronted with the impossible situation of being surrounded by poisonous snakes? (Numbers 21:7)

_____

_____

What did God tell Moses to do? (Numbers 21:8)

_____

_____

Instead of removing the snakes, God told the Israelites to do something else for protection. What were the people to do to be saved? (Numbers 21:8)

_____

3. **Overcoming the Obstacles**

Many years later Jesus referred to the experience of the Israelites and the snakes. He told Nicodemus — a man who had come inquiring about eternal life — that natural birth does not qualify a man to enter the Kingdom of Heaven; he needs to be born again of the Spirit. The purpose of being born of the Spirit is to enable a man to follow the Spirit rather than following the flesh. A Spirit-born man looks to God for all his answers, for his protection, for his provision.

What did Jesus tell Nicodemus? (John 3:14-15)

_____

_____

_____

What are the three things God commands us to do in order to qualify for His direction? (Proverbs 3:5-6)

(1) _____

_____

(2) _____

(3) _____

If we do these three things what can we expect God to do as we travel on our journey to spiritual maturity? (Proverbs 3:6)

_____

Moses realized the necessity for his people to be distinguished from all other peoples. What did Moses ask God to do to distinguish them from all the other people on the face of the earth? (Exodus 33:16)

_____

What does God promise to do when we move out on our journey toward spiritual maturity? (Exodus 33:14)

_____

4. The Need For A Guide

Although Moses was an experienced desert traveler and knew the paths through the Sinai as an expert, he knew that when the cloud moved northward toward Canaan, he would soon be in unfamiliar territory. He needed someone who could go with him, just as the Indian scouts used to accompany the wagon trains as they crossed the uncharted wilderness of the American West. He needed a guide who could find water, spot the enemy, and lead them through the maze of wadis which crisscross the northern wilderness in the Negev Desert. Moses needed a guide.

To whom did Moses turn? (Numbers 10:29)

_____

What was the guide's initial response? (Numbers 10:30)

_____

What did Moses promise his guide as a reward? (Numbers 10:32)

_____

What did Moses ask the guide to do? (Numbers 10:31)

_____

The descendants of Hobab were called Kenites. What evidence do we have that Moses' promise to Hobab was fulfilled? (Judges 1:16, I Samuel 15:6)

_____

5. God's Place In Guidance

Many years later Moses sang a ballad in which he recalled the events of his

NOTES

NOTES

wilderness wanderings. In the song he emphasized that even though he had been the earthly leader of Israel, God was their true guide. He compared the nation of Israel to a man lost in the wilderness without a guide, but said God had a special affection for the Israelites and protected the people.

What phrase does Moses use to describe Israel's relationship to God? (Deuteronomy 32:10)

_____

Moses compares God to a mother eagle. How did God treat the Israelites? (Deuteronomy 32:11-12)

_____

_____

The reference to God being an eagle brings to mind something God told Moses at Mt. Sinai. At that time God told Moses to describe God's protection.

How did God protect the Israelites? (Exodus 19:4)

_____

_____

From whom does our help come? (Psalm 121:2)

_____

How does the Psalmist describe God's protection from the heat of the wilderness? (Psalm 121:5)

_____

PERSONAL REVIEW QUESTIONS

1. T F God told Moses to follow the cloud to teach the people to obey Him daily.
2. T F The reason the Israelites wandered for 40 years was because the cloud disappeared and they couldn't find it.
3. T F God wanted the Israelites to settle down, but they insisted on moving about.
4. T F God's mercies, like His manna, are fresh every morning.
5. T F God rejoices when we grumble for it gives Him opportunity to forgive us.
6. T F We are to rejoice when we face trials and troubles.
7. T F Actually it was Satan, not God, who sent snakes to bite the people.
8. T F Moses killed a snake, nailed it to his staff, and frightened off the rest of the snakes.
9. T F Moses laid hands on the elders and they received power to pick up the snakes by the tails and turn them into staffs.
10. T F God said the only way the people would be saved from the snakes was by looking at Moses' brazen serpent.
11. T F Jesus said he must be lifted up as Moses lifted up the serpent in the wilderness.

12. T F   Since God gave us our intellect, He intends for us to learn to depend on our own understanding.
13. T F   Moses said the distinguishing differences between the Israelites and all other people on earth was the presence of God.
14. T F   Hobab was Moses' brother-in-law.
15. T F   Moses describes God as a mother eagle who pushes her little ones out of the nest to teach them how to fly.

MEMORY VERSE

John 3:14-15 (Memorize, then write it on these lines.)

_____
_____
_____
_____
_____

TRUE OR FALSE ANSWERS

1-T, 2-F, 3-F, 4-T, 5-F, 6-T, 7-F, 8-F, 9-F, 10-T, 11-T, 12-F, 13-T, 14-T, 15-T

Lesson 12
Faith: Lessons from Kadesh Barnea
God Calls Us Forward

VIDEO REFERENCE: Lesson 12

How many of us, on our journey to spiritual maturity, have gotten right to the border of the Promised Land, but for one reason or another failed to enter? The last steps of the journey are often the toughest.

The Children of Israel, after the long trek through the Sinai, finally reached the border of Canaan. It took only 11 days for them to march from Sinai to the lush oasis at Kadesh Barnea. Here God intended they should regroup, pause to be refreshed and gain strength, and then take that final step of conquest. But history records they grew fainthearted at the last minute. Fearful they could not do what God commanded, they backed down. As a result, God sentenced them to remain in the wilderness for another 40 years.

This was not God's intention. He did not want His followers to remain in the wilderness for any longer than necessary. The wilderness was simply a place of preparation, of purification. Here they received their charter for the new government, their directions for the new life they were to live. Then, equipped and marching in the power of God, they were to move on across the border and take the land God had promised them. They had already marched more than 400 miles in 15 months. They had seen God meet their every need. Surely they had learned by now that God was faithful and could be trusted. If He asked them to do something, He would provide the means to accomplish the task.

But instead of moving out with the morning's light to take the land, the people balked. It was the first step toward unbelief. Instead of acting in faith and believing God, they acted cautiously, fearing the giants and walled cities of Canaan. Instead of looking at God's promises and remembering the victories of the past, they looked at the circumstances. Like Peter walking on the water, the moment they took their eyes off

God and looked at the circumstances, their faith faltered. They received what they confessed, and their negative faith brought about their downfall.

God's Promises

God had promised them the land. He had proved Himself faithful at every turn of their journey. He could be trusted to protect them. He had said He would go before them, He would drive out the enemies which inhabited the land. He would fight their battles for them. All they had to do was go up and possess the land. "See, the Lord your God has given you the land. Go up and take possession of it as the Lord, the God of your fathers, told you. Do not be afraid; do not be discouraged" (Deuteronomy 1:21).

All it took to have what God promised was faith. A faith that said I will not be enticed away from God's best, I will not settle for the seeming safety of the wilderness, I will not turn back because of the smell of meat and onions wafting across the desert from Egypt — I will go forward . . . even if it kills me.

Instead, the Israelites decided to act cautiously. They sent spies in to scout out the land. Their report was factual. It dealt with circumstances rather than faith. It told of giants and walled cities. "We can't attack those people; they are stronger than we are . . . The land we explored devours those living in it . . . All the people are giants . . . We seemed like grasshoppers in our own eyes, and we looked the same to them." (Numbers 13:31-33) The people received this negative report, for the human heart loves to be deceived, to rebel against faith. The obstacles were too great, the menaces too many. They voted against God and opted to stay in the wilderness rather than take that final step which would insure their inheritance.

Unbelief

Unbelief never **sees** beyond the difficulties. It is always looking at walled cities and giants rather than at God. Faith looks at God; unbelief looks at obstacles. Although faith never minimizes the dangers or difficulties, it counts on God to overcome these things. The Israelites, however, looked inward at themselves. They saw themselves as grasshoppers. The more they confessed their inadequacies and inabilities, the more they accepted them as reality. They failed to do the one thing God had wanted them to do all along — look to Him as their source, rather than to their own abilites.

Many years later Jesus spoke of this same unbelief. He said He longed to perform miracles in His hometown of Nazareth but was limited because of the people's unbelief (Matthew 13:58).

On another occasion Jesus rebuked his followers who threw up their hands saying they were powerless to cast a demon out of a child. After Jesus took authority over the demon and commanded it to leave, His disciples came to Him inquiring, "Why couldn't we drive it out?" Jesus replied, "Because you have so little faith" (Matthew 17:14-20).

Perhaps the most striking example of unbelief came when Jesus got in a boat on the Sea of Galilee with His disciples. He made a simple statement: "Let us go over to the other side." He then laid down and went to sleep in the stern of the boat, leaving His disciples to row across. However, during the night a storm arose and the disciples were afraid the boat would capsize. They awoke Jesus who took authority over the wind and the waves, rebuking them and commanding the sea to be calm. He then rebuked His disciples, telling them that they had the authority to do what He had done, but because of their lack of faith they had refused to take dominion (Mark 4:35-40).

NOTES

The Sin of Unbelief

When the Israelites made their decision to refuse to enter the Promised Land, they committed the sin of unbelief. Because of this, God sentenced them to remain in the wilderness for 40 years — until all the old, unbelieving generation had died and a new generation of those who would trust God had come of age. When the Israelites realized that God meant business, that He treated willful disobedience harshly, they tried to reverse their former decision and, despite the warnings of Moses, set out to enter the Promised Land on their own. Moses pointed out that God's decision was final. The people, however, reasoned that all they had to do was reverse their previous decision. They failed to understand that genuine repentance is not so much of what we have done — but of who we are. In their case, their sin was not just their failure to possess the land. Their sin lay in their rebellion and unbelief. By attempting to reverse their former action in their own strength, they simply showed how deep their sin was, for once again they were refusing to accept God's decision.

"Do not go up, because the Lord is not with you," Moses warned them. "Because you have turned away from the Lord, He will not be with you and you will fall by the sword" (Numbers 14:42-43). However, they pushed on, trying to please God in their own strength rather than obeying Him, and many were slain by the inhabitants of Canaan and the rest were driven back into the wilderness.

God treats unbelief the same way He treats willful disobedience — for they are from the same root. It took another 40 years of waiting and wandering before a new generation was ready to obey God. All that time, God's presence remained with the Israelites in the form of the cloud by day and the pillar of fire by night. He continued to provide them with manna. His love was just as great as it was when they were obedient. But they missed His blessing — having opted for the safety of the wilderness rather than the glory of walking in faith.

CONCLUSIONS

1. Faith is essentially believing God means what He says.

2. Unbelief is a great sin, for it says God is not who He says He is.

3. Although God will continue to love and protect us, even if we disobey Him, He will withhold His best, giving that only to those who trust Him absolutely.

4. We must learn to fix our eyes — and our hearts — on God and His promises, rather than on the circumstances around us.

BIBLE STUDY

1. Obeying God's Commands

At the heart of every lesson in the wilderness is the lesson of obedience. Faith, in its basic form, is believing God is, believing God means what He says, and believing that God will fulfill His promises. It's not so much that God rewards those who believe Him; rather, those who believe Him simply receive what He has promised to all believers.

The Israelites would have been "rewarded" with the Promised Land had they been faithful to God's command to go in and possess the land. Instead they disobeyed and suffered.

What was God's original command to the Israelites concerning Canaan? (Deuteronomy 1:21)

_____

_____

_____

What prevented the Israelites from entering? (Hebrews 3:19)

_____

Twelve spies were chosen to go in and scout out the land. Upon their return they made a report to Moses.

What did the spies report to Moses? (Numbers 13:27-28)

_____

_____

_____

_____

Two of the spies gave a positive report, while the other ten gave a negative report. God sentenced the ten spies, and all the rest of the nation of Israel, to another 40 years of wandering. However, He blessed the two spies who encouraged the people to obey God and allowed them to live beyond the rest of the people and enter the Promised Land with the new generation.

What are the names of the two spies who encouraged Moses to possess the land? (Numbers 14:6-9)

_____

_____

How did the ten unfaithful spies feel when they saw the giants of Anak? (Numbers 13:33)

_____

2. **Unbelief Spawns Dissension and Rebellion**

After the ten spies made their report to Moses, they made the rounds through the camp distributing their poisonous reports. This caused the people to use worldly logic and reason and to agree with them, joining in their unbelief.

What did the people say they should do rather than go in and occupy the Promised Land? (Numbers 14:4)

_____

_____

Whom did Caleb say the people were rebelling against? (Numbers 14:9)

_____

What was God's judgment on the unbelieving Israelites? (Numbers 14:23)

_____

_____

What happened to the Israelites who went ahead and tried to occupy

NOTES

Canaan after the Lord told them to remain in the wilderness for another 40 years? (Deuteronomy 1:44)

___

3. **Jesus and Faith**

   One time Jesus was stopped by two blind men who called out to Him, asking Him to heal them. When Jesus asked them if they believed He could do it, they said yes, they believed. Jesus then touched their eyes and they received sight.

   What did Jesus say qualified them to be healed? (Matthew 9:29)

   ___

   On another occasion Jesus was teaching and some men literally removed the roof of the house. They lowered a crippled man down through the ceiling by ropes which were attached to his bed.

   What was it that impressed Jesus about this act? (Mark 2:5)

   ___

   What did Jesus say we would be able to do if we have faith? (John 14:12)

   ___

   What did Jesus say God would give us if we ask Him in the name of His Son? (John 14:14)

   ___

4. **The Quest for Faith**

   What is necessary to please God? (Hebrews 11:6)

   ___

   How are we supposed to live? (Habakkuk 2:4)

   ___

   Paul says we should not make decisions by what we see. How then are we to make decisions? (II Corinthians 5:7)

   ___

   How much faith is necessary to remove a mountain? (Matthew 17:20)

   ___

   What cancels out God's faithfulness? (Romans 3:3,4)

   ___

   How does faith come? (Romans 10:17)

   ___

   In describing the armor of God which protects the Christian from Satan, which piece did Paul relate to faith? (Ephesians 6:16)

   ___

At the end of his life Paul cherished a particular aspect of his walk with God. What did he say he had held on to? (II Timothy 4:7)

_____

What is the Biblical definition of faith? (Hebrews 11:1)

_____

_____

_____

PERSONAL REVIEW QUESTIONS

1. T F   Kadesh Barnea is the name of a city in northern Egypt.
2. T F   Moses sent 12 spies into Canaan to scout out the land.
3. T F   God was trying to teach the Israelites the democratic process — which is the model for the church — and told Moses that He would abide by the majority decision of the spies and not raise any objections.
4. T F   Only Joshua and Caleb felt the Israelites could occupy Canaan.
5. T F   Ten of the spies said the giants of Canaan were too strong for the Israelites to defeat.
6. T F   Joshua and Caleb said the Israelites were like grasshoppers in the sight of the giants.
7. T F   God condemned the ten spies because they made fun of His grasshoppers.
8. T F   The ten spies said the grasshoppers had eaten all the milk and honey in the Promised Land.
9. T F   Faith is listening to God and obeying Him.
10. T F   The Israelites could have conquered Canaan if they had exerted faith.
11. T F   Simon Peter began to sink when he was walking on water because he took his eyes off Jesus and looked at the waves.
12. T F   Jesus was able to calm the storm on the Sea of Galilee because He had read the weather report.
13. T F   God says unbelief is sin.
14. T F   It's possible to please God even if we don't have faith.
15. T F   We can do the same works as Jesus if we have faith.

MEMORY VERSE

Hebrews 11:6 (Memorize, then write it on these lines)

_____

_____

_____

TRUE OR FALSE ANSWERS

1-F, 2-T, 3-F, 4-T, 5-T, 6-T, 7-F, 8-F, 9-T, 10-T, 11-T, 12-F, 13-T, 14-F, 15-T

Lesson 13
Relationships: The Family of God
God Places His Children in Families

VIDEO REFERENCE: Lesson 13

The end result of our journey to spiritual maturity is to establish relationships — a relationship with God and a relationship with His people. The relationship with God was the one which was intended when God put the first man in the Garden of Eden. When the relationship with God was broken by sin, the relationship between men also went bad. Men and women, created to have the perfect relationship on earth in an institution called the home, were at odds with each other. In fact, all earthly relationships went sour. Men could not get along with each other. Nations warred against nations. That which was most precious to God — fellowship — was broken. God sent His Son, Jesus, to restore that relationship. As we are created in the image of Jesus, which is the purpose of our quest for spiritual maturity, we develop a new yearning for fellowship — with God and with His people.

Covenant Relationships

Covenant is the basis of all relationships. The family is a covenant relationship. The church should be a family — brothers and sisters in covenant with each other. This relationship means we have fellowship. The Greek word is *koinonia*, which means community, or fellowship. It is "family" in its purest form. It means we are loyal to each other. In fact, John said if we walk in the light — by being open and honest with each other — as God is open and honest with us, we will have *koinonia* — fellowship — with God and with His people.

God knows these relationships are best formed in times of stress and trouble. The Israelites, during their 40 years in the wilderness, came into a deep covenant relationship with God and with each other. That relationship has lasted across the centuries, passed down from generation to generation. In fact, today's Jews are an example of how that relationship still exists.

The wilderness breeds loyalty. It forces us into a camaraderie of deep covenant relationships. Thus it is not surprising God chose the wilderness to reveal His covenant nature. Covenant in its purest form is a binding and solemn agreement between individuals who have contracted for a common goal. It grows out of conflict and is always tested by suffering.

Biblical Examples

To Noah, staggered by the immensity of God's wrath, God covenanted: "I have set my rainbow in the clouds, and it will be the sign of the covenant" (Genesis 9:13).

To Abraham, wandering childless and without purpose in the desert, God covenanted: "This is my covenant with you: You will be the father of many nations" (Genesis 17:4).

Such were the convenants between God and man. But there were convenants between men of God as well. David and Jonathan had a covenant between them which made them brothers, even though separated by ideologies. The disciples of Jesus were covenanted together — formed the first church, or group of "called out ones." Barnabas had a covenant relationship with John Mark. Paul had a covenant relationship with Timothy. And today, if we move on into spiritual maturity, we shall find ourselves in relationship with other Christians who become our spiritual brothers and sisters.

The Covenant of Salt

The earliest covenant between men was called the Covenant of Salt. There is no recorded time for its beginning. It is first mentioned in Numbers 18:19 as a sign to the priests in their offerings to the Lord. "Whatever is set aside from the holy offerings... It is an everlasting covenant of salt before the Lord for both you and your offspring." Later God told the Levites to season all grain offerings with salt: "Do not leave the salt of the covenant of your God out of your grain offerings; add salt to all your offerings" (Leviticus 2:13). From the very earliest times salt was a symbol of the covenant.

To the Levites it was a sign of perpetual purity. But to the people it had a much broader meaning — a meaning preserved to this day among the Bedouin who say to each other: "There is salt between us."

Jesus and Covenant Relationships

When Jesus gathered His disciples at the beginning of His ministry He took them up on a mountain and taught them. These teachings are generally called the "Sermon on the Mount." This was not a teaching given to the general public — but to those He had "called out," the first church. He highlighted His teaching by calling them "the salt of the earth." He was speaking of this covenant of loyalty which binds men to each other in Christ. When Jesus emphasized the imperativeness of saltiness, He was referring to the necessity of walking out the covenant with God and with one another. Such covenants are forged and consummated in the crucible of wilderness experiences — and are the end of our quest for spiritual maturity. In short, Jesus said you will know you are His followers, that you have reached spiritual maturity, when you love one another enough to give your life for each other.

Covenant People

Covenant people are people who have come through the fire together. They are people loyal to one another. They are people who will die for each other. They are people who refuse to entertain malicious charges against each other. They are people who do not shoot their wounded — especially their wounded leaders. They are people who heal the sick, who love one another as brothers and sisters, who serve one another, who do not need to swear to one another because their word is their bond.

NOTES

We live in an age of easiness. We do our best to keep away from hardship. Covenants no longer exist as they should. Divorce is easier than marriage. Children are free to leave their parents. Parents desert children. Churches, which are supposed to be spiritual families, often split, often drive off their wounded. But men and women who have walked through the wilderness together have had their egos crushed. They have learned they cannot exist without God — and without each other. They have learned how to huddle. Here, in the wilderness, binding relationships are formed — the kind which never can be broken.

CONCLUSION

1. Our quest for spiritual maturity is ended when we are restored in our fellowship with God and when we love one another as Christ loved us.

2. God intends for His church to be a family of people who are loyal to each other, who treat each other as true brothers and sisters.

3. God wants each of us to be part of such a fellowship.

BIBLE STUDY

1. The Place of Covenants

Covenant is part of God's nature. It is at the heart of all His relationships. Just as the giving and receiving of wedding rings becomes the sign of a marriage, so God accompanies His covenant by some kind of sign — evidence that the covenant has been made.

What was the sign God gave Noah that he had entered into covenant with the world? (Genesis 9:13)

_____

What was God's covenant with Abraham? (Genesis 17:4)

_____

_____

What kind of covenant did God tell Ezekiel He had established with Israel? (Ezekiel 16:60)

_____

In God's Covenant with David, He promised a special blessing for David's grandchildren. What was that promise? (Psalm 132:11-12)

_____

_____

When Joshua made a covenant with the people and for the people with God, he followed God's pattern of using a sign for the covenant.

What was the sign used when he made his covenant? (Joshua 24:25-26)

_____

_____

2. **The New Covenant**

   On a number of occasions God spoke through His prophets of a covenant to come — obviously a reference to Jesus who later described Himself as "the New Covenant."

   Where did God tell Jeremiah He would place the sign of the New Covenant? (Jeremiah 31:33)

   _____

   _____

   Who is the mediator of the New Covenant? (Hebrews 12:24)

   _____

   What happened to the Old Covenant when the New Covenant appeared? (Hebrews 8:13)

   _____

   _____

3. **Covenant Relationships Bring Us Into Fellowship**

   The desire of God's heart is that we walk in fellowship with Him as Adam and Eve walked in fellowship with Him in the Garden prior to the fall. This fellowship has been restored to us through Jesus Christ.

   What kind of fellowship does God want us to have? (I Corinthians 1:9)

   _____

   We are also to have a special relationship with the Holy Spirit. How does Paul describe this? (Philippians 2:1,2)

   _____

   _____

   Wilderness experiences draw us into fellowship with God and with His people. What phrase does Paul use to describe this in Philippians 3:10?

   _____

   _____

   _____

4. **Fellowship With Each Other**

   John says that because of Jesus Christ we now have the ability to have special relationships with each other. By sharing that story this relationship is enhanced.

   With whom do we now have fellowship because of Jesus Christ? (I John 1:3)

   _____

   _____

   What happens when we walk in the light of Jesus Christ? (I John 1:7)

   (1.) _____

   (2.) _____

NOTES

NOTES

PERSONAL REVIEW QUESTIONS

1. T F The purpose of our quest for spiritual maturity is to establish a new relationship with God through Jesus.
2. T F The earliest covenant was called the Covenant of Salt.
3. T F Salt was to be included in the grain offering of the Levites.
4. T F Salt represents a binding relationship.
5. T F The family is to be a covenant relationship.
6. T F The church is the family of God.
7. T F God wants His people to be in covenant fellowship with each other and to treat each other as brothers and sisters.
8. T F Jesus is God's New Covenant with His people.
9. T F The church is the organization God has left on earth through which we can have fellowship with each other.
10. T F Walking in the light is mandatory if we are to have fellowship with each other.
11. T F If we walk in the light we'll not only have fellowship with each other, but with God.
12. T F We know we have attained spiritual maturity when we love each other enough to die for each other.

MEMORY VERSE
I John 1:7 (Memorize, then write it on these lines.)

_____

_____

_____

TRUE OR FALSE ANSWERS:
1-T, 2-T, 3-T, 4-T, 5-T, 6-T, 7-T, 8-T, 9-T, 10-T, 11-T, 12-T

ABOUT JAMIE BUCKINGHAM

A master story-teller and Bible teacher, Jamie Buckingham has delighted millions around the world both in person and in print.

He wrote more than 45 books, including biographies of some of this century's best known Christians, including Pat Robertson (*Shout It from the Housetops*), Corrie ten Boom (*Tramp for the Lord* and others), and Kathryn Kuhlman (*Daughter of Destiny, God Can Do it Again* and others). His other biographies include the national best seller *Run Baby Run* (with Nicky Cruz), *From Harper Valley to the Mountaintop* (with Jeannie C. Riley), and *O Happy Day* (the Happy Goodman Family Singers). Other books by Jamie Buckingham include *Risky Living, Into the Glory* (about the jungle aviator branch of Wycliffe Bible Translators); *Where Eagles Soar* (a sequel to *Risky Living*); *A Way Through the Wilderness*; *Coping With Criticism*, and *Jesus World* (a novel). He also wrote *Power for Living*, a book sponsored by the Arthur DeMoss Foundation that was given away to millions of people worldwide and resulted in untold numbers of people coming to Christ.

Jamie was more than an author of books. He was an award-winning columnist for *Charisma Magazine* and served as Editor-in-Chief of *Ministries Today* magazine until his death in February of 1992.

A popular conference speaker, he was recognized as one of America's foremost authorities on the Sinai and Israel. He wrote and produced more than 100 video teachings on location in the Holy Land.

As a distinguished Bible teacher with graduate degrees in English Literature and Theology, Jamie was respected among liturgical, evangelical, and Pentecostal Christians. He was a close friend and confidant of many key Christians of the late 20th century, including Oral Roberts, Billy Graham, Catherine Marshall, Jack Hayford, Bob Mumford, Kathryn Kuhlman, Corrie ten Boom, John Sherrill, Bill Bright, John Hagee, Pat Robertson, and many others.

Most importantly, Jamie was a husband, father, grandfather, and founding pastor of the Tabernacle Church, an interdenominational congregation in Melbourne, Florida, where he served for 25 years, pastoring and discipling followers of Christ. He lived in a rural area on the east coast of Florida on a family compound with his wife, Jackie, surrounded by five married children and 14 grandchildren.

For more information on Jamie Buckingham please visit www.JamieBuckinghamMinistries.com. Many of his books, columns, additional writings, video devotional series, and audio sermons can be found on this website, which is dedicated to preserving his life works.

You can also order Jamie's book *Spiritual Maturity*, based on this workbook and video series, as well as his classic book, *A Way Through The Wilderness*, from which this video series and workbook was inspired.

For more of Jamie Buckingham's books, teachings and devotionals, or if you would like additional copies of this workbook, go to:

www.JamieBuckinghamMinistries.com

Other video devotionals by Jamie Buckingham include:

10 Miracles of Jesus
10 Bible People Like Me
10 Parables of Jesus
Armed for Spiritual Warfare
50 Days Before Easter

Risky Living Ministries, Inc.

www.RLMin.com

Made in United States
Orlando, FL
13 July 2023

35072108R00057